Headline Series

No. 286   **FOREIGN POLICY ASSOCIATION** $4.00

The Politics of International Sport— Games of Power

by Wallace Irwin Jr.

Cover Design: Ed Bohon   Nov./Dec. 1987
                                                Published August 1988

The Author

WALLACE IRWIN JR. became acquainted with
world politics and U.S. foreign policy through
graduate study at Princeton University, staff work
in the U.S. Senate and 14 years as public affairs
adviser and principal speech writer at the U.S.
Mission to the United Nations. He was a staff
officer on the U.S. delegation to the UN Conference
on the Human Environment in Stockholm, Sweden,
in 1972. After leaving government service in 1972
he became a freelance writer and editor of the
annual *Issues Before the General Assembly,* published by the United Nations Association of the
U.S.A., and other publications on the UN, then
served four years as chief editor at the Foreign
Policy Association. He is the author of *America in*

the World: A Guide to U.S. Foreign Policy. He and his wife live in Larchmont,
New York, where he is active on many local and regional environmental issues.

The Foreign Policy Association

The Foreign Policy Association is a private, nonprofit, nonpartisan educational
organization. Its purpose is to stimulate wider interest and more effective
participation in, and greater understanding of, world affairs among American
citizens. Among its activities is the continuous publication, dating from 1935, of
the HEADLINE SERIES. The author is responsible for factual accuracy and for the
views expressed. FPA itself takes no position on issues of U.S. foreign policy.

HEADLINE SERIES (ISSN 0017-8780) is published five times a year, January, March,
May, September and November, by the Foreign Policy Association, Inc., 729
Seventh Ave., New York, N.Y. 10019. Chairman, Robert V. Lindsay; President, John
W. Kiermaier; Editor in Chief, Nancy L. Hoepli; Senior Editor, Ann R. Monjo;
Associate Editor, K. M. Rohan. Subscription rates, $15.00 for 5 issues; $25.00 for 10
issues; $30.00 for 15 issues. Single copy price $4.00. Discount 25% on 10 to 99 copies;
30% on 100 to 499; 35% on 500 to 999; 40% on 1,000 or more. Payment must
accompany orders for $8 or less. Add $1.50 for postage. Second-class postage paid at
New York, N.Y. POSTMASTER: Send address changes to HEADLINE SERIES, Foreign
Policy Association, 729 Seventh Ave., New York, N.Y. 10019. Copyright 1988 by
Foreign Policy Association, Inc. Composed and printed at Science Press, Ephrata,
Pennsylvania.

Library of Congress Catalog Card No. 88-82097
ISBN 0-87124-121-8

1

A Marriage of Convenience

- *Mexico City, Apr. 21, 1968: Black African countries drop boycott, send top athletes to the Olympic Games after Olympic officials and Mexican government ban South Africa.*
- *Munich, Sept. 5, 1972: Palestinian terrorists break into Olympic Village, kidnap and kill 11 Israeli athletes.*
- *Moscow, July 19, 1980: U.S. and 61 other countries boycott first summer Olympic Games ever held in a Communist country to protest Soviet invasion of Afghanistan.*
- *Los Angeles, July 28, 1984: A record 140 countries participate in summer Olympics, but the Soviet Union and most of its allies stay away.*
- *Indianapolis, Aug. 8, 1987: A 500-member team from Cuba arrives here for Pan American Games.*

The above are a few of countless illustrations of the perpetual interaction of international sport and international politics. These two dimensions of life are so very different—the exhilarating realm of sport and the ruthless political game of power. Is such a marriage of seeming incompatibles a good thing? Baron

Pierre de Coubertin of France, who started the modern Olympic Games in the 1890s, thought not. He passionately believed that the noble realm of sport should, if it touched the political world at all, contribute to peace and understanding among nations—and must never be contaminated with grosser elements of power politics and national rivalry. Later his American disciple Avery Brundage, the high priest of the Olympics for two decades, railed constantly against departures from that shining ideal. But it was a losing battle; indeed, the very structure and symbolism of the Olympics, with national teams, flags and anthems, guaranteed from the outset that national politics would have its say.

An Inevitable Linkage

Indeed, like it or not, the linkage of sport and politics has existed from ancient times, and is probably inevitable. The reasons why are not mysterious:

▶ For spectators as well as players, games—especially team sports which evoke intense group loyalties—are among the great enjoyments of life, and are extremely popular, more so than ever now that television has multiplied a millionfold the number of seats in the audience. And whatever is popular is politically important.

▶ In modern democracies, sport is an important leveler—a chance for the best to excel, regardless of color or class.

▶ Sport promotes physical fitness—a factor in calculations of national power.

▶ Success in the international sporting arena enhances a nation's pride at home and its prestige abroad.

▶ And not least important, the popularity of sports makes them good business—a weighty consideration for politicians in any modern country, whether business is in private hands or in the hands of the state.

Any statesman would have to be exceptionally obtuse not to make political use of the games people are so addicted to—whether soccer or baseball or Korean "martial arts" or the Malaysian kickball favorite called *sepak takraw*. In the Soviet Union, China and other countries where power is highly central-

4

Seoul, host city of the XXIVth Summer Olympics, September 1988

ized—and, for that matter, in many pluralistic democracies, with the conspicuous exception of the United States—governments identify, train and support the most promising athletes; assist and guide national sport organizations in Olympic and other international competition; and play host to international sporting events. In black Africa, where young nations strive against age-old ethnic and cultural divisions, leaders have sought to mold a sense of nationhood by making heroes of their champions like Ethiopia's great marathoner, Abebe Bekila, or Kenya's middle-distance prodigy, Kipchoge Keino.

As for the United States, one need only recall how the entire U.S. Olympic hockey team, fresh from their underdog victory over the Soviet champions in the 1980 winter Olympics at Lake Placid, New York, got a heroes' welcome at the White House from the President himself. That glamorous moment was probably valued by Jimmy Carter as much as by the athletes, hard-pressed as he then was by the Iran hostage crisis, the Soviet invasion of Afghanistan, and his approaching campaign for reelection.

And consider the multiple political values that the leaders of the Republic of Korea (South Korea) gain from holding the 1988 summer Olympics in the capital city of Seoul. The event sends the world a signal that this country long classed as "developing" is now an industrial power and an important trading partner. And it marks an advance in world prestige for South Korea as against its hostile North Korean neighbor, whose attempts either to share or sabotage the Seoul Olympics have won little support.

Different Aims, Mutual Need

In these pages we shall examine that often perplexing dimension of international sport—the marriage between sport and politics. It is an uncomfortable marriage, strained by purposes that often conflict.

Sport, for spectators as well as players, is a specially prized part of living. For most of us, life without it wouldn't be much fun. True, some artists and intellectuals despise it—John Mortimer, the English playwright, novelist and barrister, hated it from childhood and insists that it "fosters international hostility and leads the audience, no doubt from boredom, to do grievous bodily harm while watching it." But others, like the poet and avid baseball fan Marianne Moore, have doted on it and written poems about it. Sport fulfills not only physical but psychological needs—the aesthetic need for beauty in action and, perhaps even more potent, the competitive need to win. Yet, no matter how fiercely competitive the game becomes, winner and loser are bound by an agreed set of rules; and although the stakes include money for some, glory or shame for many, they do not—in today's world at least—include life and death or territorial conquest. Sport is many things to many people; it sometimes even leads to small-scale bloodshed; but it is not war. The loser lives to play again.

Politics, by contrast, if it can be called a game at all, is a desperately serious one. It is played on fields as small as an office or a village hall, or as vast as the planet and even outer space. Its chief players are the independent (yet interdependent) states that make up the world political system. Politics too has agreed rules which are more or less obeyed, but its supreme rule is power. Most of us put up with it not because it is enjoyable (although for some the power and glory it brings are the supreme enjoyments of life) but because the alternatives, anarchy and war, are worse. Wielding the power of the law, the purse and the gun, politicians can go far to determine success or failure, even life or death, across the entire range of human activity, including sport.

In its marriage with sport, therefore, politics is obviously the senior partner. Luckily, however, politicians more often than not take a positive view of sports, often exploiting them for political ends but hardly ever suppressing them. The reason is clear: sports are popular. The instinct of play, especially competitive play, is so universal, so essential to human felicity, that it has a power and necessity of its own.

Just what makes sports so popular is a deep question, but part of the answer must be their easy accessibility. Far more than the fine arts or the life of the intellect, sports can be enjoyed, either physically or vicariously, by vast numbers of people without the need for years of tiresome study. Also, some authorities say, competitive sports provide a relatively harmless way of satisfying the fighting urge that is built into most of us whether by our genes or our conditioning or both.

Whatever the reasons, there seem to be few other human activities—one thinks of mass demonstrations in times of crisis, or ecstatic religious or cult gatherings under charismatic leaders—that can pack in 80,000 or more cheering and shouting spectators, with hundreds of millions more watching on TV. Brundage once described the Olympic Movement as "a twentieth-century religion, a religion with universal appeal which incorporates all the basic values of other religions, a modern, exciting, virile, dynamic religion." Discounting the effusive rhetoric, the words contain a grain of truth.

It is above all that fact of popularity, intensified to the point of extreme devotion (witness the origin of the word "fan" from "fanatic") that solidly links the world of sport to the world of politics. It was so in the age of the original Greek Olympics, held every four years with much religious pomp for many centuries by the Greek city-states. Still more is it so in today's world of popular nationalism, global business deals, jet travel and live-by-satellite TV. Now, in fact, the political significance of sport is worldwide.

Seen in this perspective, international sports are one dimension of a still vaster game whose players include not only athletes, coaches, team owners and fans, but industrialists, advertisers, consumers, TV executives, legislators, middlemen, bureaucrats, politburos, presidents, prime ministers, kings and queens. The stakes are not just Olympic gold but national power, pride, prestige and profit.

The story has its quota of hypocrisy, bad taste, bad manners, drugs, bribery, primitive violence, even terrorism. But it also tells of magnanimity, brilliant achievement, strong bonds of friendship and respect across national lines, and the sheer joy and beauty of great performances. To look at world sport through the lens of world politics, as we are about to do, can increase our understanding of both. It can also raise worthwhile questions about the role of the United States: specifically, how American decisionmakers in the interconnected fields of foreign policy and international sport deal with their common concerns, and how they might do better.

2

From Primitive Cult
to Olympic Gold

Something deep in human nature seems to need to play games. The sociologist Günther Lüschen calls sport "one of the few cross-cultural universals" found in all known cultures past or present, no matter how primitive. Its character varies widely from one people to another and is not always competitive. Among Eskimos in Canada, wrestling and other games are essentially cooperative, yielding no prize except honor, but valued as entertainment and as training for survival in the hostile Arctic environment. A noncompetitive spirit prevails also in the Polynesian cultures of the Pacific islands. A story is told of a European in one such peaceable culture who coached the local young men in footracing. At the word "Go!" all the runners sprang from their starting blocks, joined hands, ran like mad, and crossed the finish line together.

Most sport, however, is intensely competitive. Much of it is more or less violent. Some games, in fact, serve as training for that ultimate competition, war. Plato, living in an age of chronic strife among the Greek city-states, advised concerning gymnastic contests in his ideal state that "only the warlike sort of them are to be practiced and to have prizes of victory; and those which are not military are to be given up." Under the Roman emperors, writes historian Allen Guttmann, the essence of sport was fighting and fitness for war—plus entertainment for a mass public addicted to brutality. In fourteenth-century England, competition with the longbow among yeomen archers received royal encouragement and proved its devastating effect against French armies in the decisive battles of Crécy and Agincourt. The warlike Sioux Indians prized competitive games and honored the winners as highly as their best hunters and warriors. In our own time, the routine mayhem in professional hockey and occasional bloody riots such as those triggered by English hooligans at European soccer matches in 1985 and 1988 remind us that players as well as spectators can often be aroused to violence.

Does this mean that sports actually foster aggression? The ethologist Konrad Lorenz, in his book *On Aggression,* thought not; rather, he maintained, they are a constructive, peaceful, rule-bound outlet for our inborn aggressive tendencies. Sport, he wrote, "educates man to a conscious and responsible control of his own fighting behavior." In a similar vein, the apostles of the modern Olympic Games have always insisted that Olympic rivalries are an influence for peace and friendship among nations. Whether this is true or false, or part way between, would seem to depend on the values of the players and fans—values that vary widely among different cultures.

Sacred Games, Royal Games

In many if not most prescientific societies, games have been closely tied to the religious rites by which the people seek to win the favor of the gods. The Navajo Indians have a god of footracing. Races and other sports are part and parcel of the fertility rites of the Apache, by which the sun god is persuaded to cause crops to grow and women to bear children. Even in our time, Zulu soccer teams in South Africa, even though professionally coached and playing by international federation rules, spend the night before a big game in an elaborate series of magic rituals led by their witch doctor or *Inyanga;* and if the team has a bad season it is more likely to be the Inyanga, not the coach, who gets fired.

Royalty and aristocracy, as well as the priestly class, have often played a special, and highly privileged, part in the sports of preindustrial peoples. In Tahiti, archery was long treated as a sacred sport, too noble for ordinary folk and practiced only by the "chieftain clans" who dominated the island; and in Polynesian sailing races it was well understood that the front-running boat, that of the king, was never overtaken. Formerly among the Baganda of East Africa, it was said that when the king wrestled, anybody defeating him would be killed. In England under King Henry VIII and King James I, bowling and tennis were sports reserved for the aristocracy. As late as 1879, when the famous annual rowing regatta at Henley, England, was founded, the rules forbade participation by anybody who was or ever had been "a mechanic, artisan, or laborer."

The First Olympics

The Greeks were not the only people of ancient times, nor even the first, to give athletic games a prominent place in their culture. The Tailteann Games of Ireland, founded in honor of a pre-Christian goddess, go back 3,000 years—perhaps the earliest regularly celebrated athletic festival. Depictions of athletic contests are found in the royal tombs at Beni Hassan in Egypt, nearly 4,000 years old; and among the carvings on the thousand-year-old Mayan ruins in Mexico are scenes of athletes playing some sort of football.

The Greek games, however, are uniquely significant in history both as marking a transition between primitive and modern sport and as a prime source of inspiration and symbolism for the modern Olympics. Founded, according to legend, in 776 B.C., the Greek Olympics were celebrated every four years, with solemn religious rites, in the vicinity of the temple of Zeus at Olympia. They drew contestants and spectators from city-states all over the Greek-speaking world, extending eastward along the coast of

11

what is now Turkey and westward as far as Massilia (present-day Marseilles). At first consisting of a single footrace, the program soon included boxing, wrestling, horse and chariot races and many other sports. Only Greeks were allowed to compete.

Similar athletic festivals were held in other Greek city-states of that era, but the Olympics were the first and the most famous. They continued for over a thousand years, long outlasting Greek civilization's golden age, but were so corrupted and brutalized under the Roman empire that the Christian emperors put a stop to them. In their heyday, the games reflected not only the Greeks' enthusiasm for the physical grace and power of the human body, but also—and equally significant—a political sense of the unity of Greek civilization. Divided though they were among small, often warring states, all Greeks shared one language and religious tradition and thought their culture superior to all others. Their Homeric legend told how, centuries earlier, all Greeks together had fought against Troy. From the fifth century B.C. well into the Olympic age, Persian invaders interrupted the Greeks' quarrels and united them again. The Olympics gave expression to this fragile but deeply felt unity. Always during the games, states at war granted safe conduct for participants to and from the games under a "sacred truce."

But whether in peace or war, competing athletes clashed in intense rivalry. Wrestling and boxing matches were sometimes fought until one contestant was dead, or nearly so. Winners were crowned with olive wreaths and showered with gifts by their patrons. (The word "athlete" derives from the Greek *athlon,* meaning prize.) There was little sympathy for losers. Pindar, the great poet of the Greek games, wrote in praise of a boy wrestling champion from Aegina:

> . . . you pinned four wrestlers
> unrelentingly, and sent
> them home in losers' gloom;
> no pleasant laughter cheered them as they reached
> their mothers' sides; shunning ridicule,
> they took to alleys, licking losers' wounds.

Bangladesh: U.S. coach Remi Korchemny, a former Soviet citizen, prepares athletes for the 1986 Junior Asian Games. He helped them win their first medals in international competition.

This cult of winners and heroes was also a cult of the rich, the powerful and the elect. By modern standards, the Greeks of Olympian days were no democrats. Chariot races, the subject of many of Pindar's Olympian odes, could be afforded only by kings and men of wealth. Slaves and women were altogether excluded from the games. Women, in fact, were forbidden even to watch, and eventually organized their own games, called the *Heraea*.

Sport in the Modern World

Like many other aspects of modern civilization, sport as we know it today evolved chiefly in Europe and the New World in the eighteenth and nineteenth centuries. This was an age of scientific rationalism, national wars, the decline of royal and ecclesiastical power, the growth of industry, technology, transport, communication, literacy, big cities and labor unions and the gradual, occasionally violent, democratizing of political life. The German *Turnverein* (gymnastic union) movement was one of the

13

athletic innovations of that era, inspired by nationalist fervor against Napoleon's imperial rule; it played a part in the rise of modern Germany. Similarly, in the Sokol movement that spread among the oppressed Czechs beginning in the 1880s, gymnastics went hand in hand with nationalist resistance to the rule of imperial Austria. Elsewhere, more-technology-minded sport enthusiasts emphasized scientific training for track and field and other competitive sports. They standardized rules and kept elaborate statistics. The word "record" began to be used to mean the best performance yet recorded in a given event.

Some sports, especially in England, remained largely the province of the upper class; others were popularized by labor unions, trade groups and religious and political organizations. It was in this way that English football evolved in the mid-nineteenth century into two distinct games—rugby, the game of the public school and university élite, and "association football" (soccer), started by university students but rapidly popularized and destined to become the most popular sport on earth. Especially in Germany, the rise of the labor movement after 1890 led to the popularizing of organized sports among the German working class.

Still, a leading place in the sporting world was held by the European nobility—a cosmopolitan class whose political dominance had declined but whose members had leisure, money and many friendships and bonds of kinship across international boundaries. It was natural for them to disdain the paid professional athlete. Instead they embraced the ideal—popularized in England in the mid-nineteenth century by *Tom Brown's School Days,* Thomas Hughes' novel about life at Rugby School—of the gentleman sportsman who competes purely for the love of the sport, valuing good manners and fair play even more than winning. In politics, it was equally natural for members of this privileged class to temper their national loyalties with a wider international view, favorable to peace and the status quo and opposed to the popular nationalist passions that can lead to war.

These aristocratic tendencies powerfully influenced the beginnings of the next great innovation in sport history, the modern

Olympic Games. Over time, however, as we shall see, the Olympic framework proved to have no magic by which to control the politics of nationalism; and as for the amateur ideal, the inexorable forces of competition in sport, politics and business gradually rendered it virtually obsolete.

De Coubertin and the Olympic Revival

The revival in 1896 of the ancient Olympic Games, which had been dead for some 1,500 years, was primarily the achievement of Baron de Coubertin. An educator with a passion for sports, he took France's humiliating defeat by a newly powerful Germany in the war of 1870–71 as a warning that the French had gone soft for the lack of a strong program of physical training. De Coubertin was a patriot—*ludus pro patria* (play for your country) was his motto—but no chauvinist. He concluded that peaceful athletic competition with other nations would improve the physical condition and national morale of the French. He also argued that an international sport festival, regularly held, would contribute to friendship and peace among the world's youth. He traveled to England and the United States for inspiration, and—none too realistically—adopted as his own the English notion of the gentleman amateur athlete. To this day, Rule 3 of the Olympic Rules and Regulations embodies those high-minded concepts: "The aims of the Olympic Movement are to promote the development of those fine physical and moral qualities which are the basis of amateur sport and to bring together the athletes of the world in a great quadrennial festival of sports thereby creating international respect and goodwill and thus helping to construct a better and more peaceful world."

De Coubertin's most arresting idea was to appropriate for his proposed festival the name and glamour—and the four-year cycle—of the Olympic Games of ancient Greece, whose history he had long studied and admired. In 1894 he convened in Paris the original International Olympic Committee (IOC), composed of sport-loving aristocrats from countries of Europe and North and South America. They endorsed his project, but it met with problems elsewhere. Most Frenchmen found it uninteresting.

Some sport federations, especially the gymnasts, viewed it as an attempt to take them over. And Athens, which for symbolic reasons was to serve as host to the first modern Olympics, at first showed little enthusiasm for this costly honor.

Fortunately, a wealthy Greek businessman volunteered to pay for rebuilding Athens' ancient stadium; and strong support came from Greece's young Crown Prince Constantine, a keen athlete and a born showman, glad of the chance to popularize himself in Greece despite his Danish ancestry. Under his chairmanship, and with de Coubertin the master organizer, the first modern Olympic Games were held in Athens in April 1896. Nearly three quarters of the athletes were Greek; the 81 foreigners—all male, none a world-class athlete—came from a mere 13 countries, all European except for 14 Americans and one Chilean. There were 42 events in track and field, pistol shooting, fencing, gymnastics, wrestling, weight-lifting, tennis, swimming and bicycling. The event most symbolic of the Olympics, then as ever afterward, was the marathon. Appropriately, it was won by a Greek peasant who was promptly showered with royal gifts. (The first marathon ever run, it was invented and financed for the occasion by a French benefactor who loved the classic flavor of a favorite schoolbook legend—a Greek soldier's heroic run from Marathon to Athens in 490 B.C. with news of victory over the invading Persians. There was no such race in the ancient Olympics.)

De Coubertin's dream had come true, in high style if somewhat amateurishly. Plans for future games went forward—but with poor results at first. In Paris in 1900, and again in St. Louis in 1904, the Olympics were confusingly jumbled in with concurrent world's fairs; and besides, St. Louis was too costly for most European athletes to reach by ship and rail. London, the host in 1908, put on a better show in which British athletes won the lion's share of medals—an emotional boost for England after its disastrous Boer War in South Africa, but the cause of bitter American complaints that British judges had been biased. Not until 1912 in Stockholm, a brilliant show with more than 2,500 athletes from 28 countries, did the future of the modern Olympics seem assured—none too soon, or the Olympic Movement might have been snuffed out by World War I. The year 1916 was marked not by the planned Sixth Olympic Games in Berlin, but by mass slaughter on the battlefields of France and rumblings of the coming revolution in Russia. In those prewar years of trial and error some important Olympic precedents had been established.

▶ An elaborate opening ceremonial, begun at Athens in 1896 and further developed in subsequent *Olympiads* (the quadrennial Olympic celebrations) was adopted to symbolize Olympic ideals: the opening of the games by the head of state of the host country; the release of a flight of doves; the singing of an Olympic hymn; the raising of the Olympic flag with its famous five linked rings, symbolizing the five continents; the taking of an Olympic oath by the leading athlete of the host country on behalf of all participants; and, perhaps most famous of all, the lighting of the Olympic flame after a torch relay of thousands of runners (linked nowadays by air across the oceans) all the way from Olympia, Greece.

▶ From the outset, internationalism notwithstanding, athletes were chosen as representatives of their respective countries and competed under their national flags. Ever since, the steady elaboration of national symbolism at the Olympics—flags, uniforms, anthems and the like—has competed with, indeed often drowned out, the themes of internationalism.

▶ Ignoring classical Greece's male supremacy, the modern Olympics—not without controversy—began to include women's events as early as 1900. By the 1930s the fame of such star performers as Sonja Henie, Norway's great figure skater, and Mildred (Babe) Didrikson, the American track and field star, had established women's sports as a permanent feature of the Olympics. Today all but a handful of sports in the summer and winter Olympics feature women's as well as men's events, and the names of outstanding athletes like Wilma Rudolph and Katarina Witt are as famous as those of their male counterparts.

▶ Amateurism, though impossible to define, became deeply entrenched as part of the Olympic ideology—the most painful proof occurring in 1913 when the great Jim Thorpe of the United

States was required to hand back the three gold medals he had won at Stockholm in track and field events after admitting that he had once earned $25 a week playing semi-pro baseball. Only much later did the IOC's strict rules on amateur standing lose their force.

▶ Despite Greece's aspiration—maintained off and on to this day—to be permanent host to the Olympics, it was established that successive Olympics would be hosted at four-year intervals by different cities chosen by the IOC from among those applying.

▶ The IOC—led by de Coubertin, who remained president until 1925—gained acceptance as the sole authority with power to grant or withhold recognition of each nation's Olympic committee, which in turn would assemble its national team. The IOC also had the power to pick the site for each quadrennial festival and to accept or reject sports or events proposed for inclusion. Moreover, the IOC became a self-perpetuating body, electing congenially upper-class members from countries deemed significant in the world of sport—virtually all of them Western except Japan—and insisting that these members were "ambassadors" from the IOC to their own countries, not the other way around.

The Interwar Years

All these precedents were adhered to during the Olympiads of the interwar years, when the summer games were held in Antwerp (1920), Paris (1924), Amsterdam (1928), Los Angeles (1932) and, under the Nazi banners of Adolf Hitler, in Berlin (1936). But those years saw many changes too, reflecting still greater changes in the world political environment. Russia, an Olympic participant since 1908, had been revolutionized by Lenin's Bolsheviks, and neither sought nor received invitations to the "bourgeois" Olympics of the interwar decades. But the Olympic Movement expanded elsewhere, welcoming IOC members from India (1920, despite its colonial status), China (1922) and Iran (1924). This trend reflected another phenomenon of that era—the rapid spread of Western culture and political forms to the non-Western world. In 1915, with the 1916 Olympics cancelled, the IOC made itself useful by sponsoring the Far Eastern Games—a forerunner of today's quadrennial Asian Games, and the IOC's first venture into regional games sponsorship. And in 1936 the IOC awarded the 1940 Olympic hostship to Japan, the first non-Western country to be so honored. But soon Japan, bent on its wars of conquest, withdrew its hostship offer. (In 1939 Finland, the IOC's second choice, was invaded by the Soviets. By then World War II was on, and the games were cancelled for the duration.)

Another innovation of this period, promoted mainly by the Scandinavians, was the Olympic winter games, instituted at Chamonix, France, in 1924. In a gesture to warm-weather countries, the winter Olympics were not counted as part of the official Olympiad; but they grew steadily in participation and popularity, and the distinction has little importance. They have been held ever since during the winter immediately preceding the summer Olympics; however, beginning in 1994 the winter and summer games will alternate at two-year intervals.

As the games grew in prestige, they became a world stage on which rival nations could earn glory through the exploits of their athletes and, on occasion, through being host country. Patriotic interest in the Olympics was whetted not only by the official display of flags and anthems but by unofficial compilations of national point scores, showing which country had "won" the games in a certain year—a practice accurately reflecting the psychology of our nationalistic age and widely covered by news media.

Seldom has this nationalistic element been more flagrantly in evidence than at the 1936 Olympics in Germany. When the IOC in 1931 chose Berlin for the 1936 summer games, it was a sign that the victors in World War I were ready at last to readmit Germany—at that point a rather shaky republic—into polite international society. But only two years later the republic fell victim to the Nazi dictatorship of Hitler, of whose demonic genius most people in Europe and America were only beginning to be aware. Hitler shrewdly ignored some advisers who saw the Olympics as a toy of the degenerate democracies and urged him to cancel them. Instead, on the advice of his propaganda minister, Paul Joseph Goebbels, he ordered that the Berlin Olympics be used as a world stage to glorify the Nazi state and the superiority of the German "race."

In the United States and elsewhere, the coming Berlin Olympics became the focus of a raging debate concerning Nazi Germany's anti-Semitism, especially after its adoption of the draconian Nuremberg Laws of 1935. Some leaders, Christian as well as Jewish, demanded a boycott of the games. But the prevailing view in the IOC—and among American Olympic leaders, including Brundage, the IOC's future president—was antiboycott. So the nations that were to be in a mortal struggle with Nazi Germany only a few years later overrode the objectors and sent large teams to Berlin. The games, held in a grandiose setting of Nazi pomp, brought Germans the biggest share of medals and went far to fulfill Hitler's propaganda wish—except for a few jarring notes, including the winning of four gold medals by a black man, the dazzling American track and field star Jesse Owens.

The presence at the Berlin games of a record 3,000 journalists reflected the political and ideological tension pervading this spectacle quite as much as its undoubted importance in the history of sport. Significantly, too, the Berlin games were the first Olympics to be broadcast internationally by shortwave radio—a small foretaste of the immense role that a still more potent medium, television, would one day play in the drama, business and politics of international sport.

3

1945–88: World Sport
in a Turbulent Age

● *Seoul, Republic of Korea, July 1953: Armistice in divided Korea has silenced the guns, but this ancient capital city, devastated at the outset of the three-year war, is a scene of utter ruin.*

● *Seoul, summer 1988: This booming capital of the pro-Western Republic of Korea expects to welcome athletes from 161 nations—probably not including North Korea—to the gala opening of the XXIVth Summer Olympics in September.*

The dramatic change revealed by these two snapshots of Korea, 35 years apart, is but one detail in the global transformations that followed World War II. In the world's industrial North, rival superpower alliances became locked in a seemingly interminable global cold war and a nuclear arms race. In the less-developed South, until then largely under colonial rule, the huge empires of the West dissolved into an expanded community of independent nations covering nearly all the world. Worldwide, these four decades saw explosive population growth and massive migration from country to city; revolutionary advances in travel, transport and mass communication, including television; and increases in world trade and investment to unheard-of levels. Hundreds of local wars, and countless acts of protest, terrorism and repression, arose from conflicts over power, wealth and national or ethnic aspirations. Everywhere there were new encounters, some friendly and some violent, between mutually ignorant cultures and religions.

World Sport Comes of Age

It was in such conditions of turbulent change that world sports, including the Olympic Games, attained their present stature. Before World War II, the largest number of countries with teams competing in the Olympics was 46 (Amsterdam, 1928). By 1964, when decolonization reached full flood, the number had grown to 94; by 1984, to 140, a record that would be exceeded again four years later. Most of the new participants were newly independent states of the Third World. (Also included, following a long Olympic tradition, are a number of colonies and dependencies, including Guam, the U.S. Virgin Islands, the Netherlands Antilles and the self-governing Commonwealth of Puerto Rico.)

The same trend is seen in the changing makeup of the IOC. In 1936 the IOC members from Europe, the old "white" Commonwealth and North America made up three quarters of the membership. Although some of their countries were, or would soon be, under totalitarian rule (Germany, Italy, Spain, Hungary), the majority were representative democracies. All had a small sport-loving upper class from which most leaders of international sport were recruited. The remaining quarter of the members were evenly divided between Latin America and Asia—and included a Japanese prince, a Japanese count and an Egyptian pasha. The only member from the African continent was from white-ruled South Africa. The world's only Communist country, the Soviet Union, was still outside the Olympic pale.

By 1987, the IOC, like the world, had been transformed. Members from the Western group made up barely over two fifths of the total; nearly half were from Asia, Africa and Latin America, and on many issues these could count on the nine votes of the Soviet-bloc members. The shift sufficed to tip the scales on important issues facing the IOC—notably those concerning South Africa, now ostracized from the Olympic system.

Players in the Game

Many of the political battles in the postwar international sport world have taken the form of disputes over organization. To understand them, it is necessary to look briefly at the way in which world sport is organized.

At the summit of the sport world sits the IOC. But, unlike Zeus of old, the IOC has few thunderbolts to command obedience. Instead it must negotiate, mainly with several kinds of official bodies:

(1) A growing number of international sport federations, each governing competition in a particular sport such as track and field, basketball, boxing, rowing, ice hockey, weight-lifting, judo, etc. Each federation, in turn, works with the appropriate national federation in each member country—for example, in the United States, the Athletic Congress for track and field sports, the USA Amateur Boxing Federation for boxing, etc. The American organizations, and their counterparts in numerous other democracies, are genuinely nongovernmental; but in most countries they are controlled or influenced by the state.

(2) The national Olympic committee (NOC) in each participating country. This body—in the United States it is the U.S. Olympic Committee—works with domestic sport organizations to oversee the selection, training and financing of the nation's entire Olympic team. In some countries the NOC is virtually a government agency; in others, including the United States, government interference is rare.

(3) The host city Olympic organizing committee in charge of site preparations for the next Olympics. Preparation begins the minute the IOC "awards" the games for a certain year—normally six years ahead of time—and continues until those particular games are over.

Conspicuously absent from the above list are key players in the Olympic drama: the athletes, their innumerable fans, business firms and governments. Officially, the IOC has little direct contact with any of these. But all of them are essential to the functioning of international sport.

Athletes and Fans

Training and, in large measure, selection of Olympic athletes rests with sport federations at the national level. The Swedish cross-country skiers at Calgary in 1988, for example, were chosen by the national ski organization in Sweden, which in turn must conform to rules laid down by the Fédération Internationale du Ski. Seldom has the IOC involved itself directly with individual athletes—and then only in futile attempts to discipline them for infractions of its "amateur" rules, a function it now leaves mainly to the international federations. For their part, Olympic athletes live to compete, and—when not inhibited by government subsidies—often object strongly to political actions that prevent them from doing so.

The fans exert a constant and pervasive, though indirect, pressure on the entire system. Only their enthusiasm can justify the heavy expenditures that make international sports possible. Therefore the Olympics, to sustain that enthusiasm against the competition of, for example, national professional sports, must include the greatest performers; must allow scope for patriotic emotion; and must see to it that Olympic host cities seat enough spectators and provide facilities for world TV and print media coverage. Actions that interfere with these needs damage the Olympics in the eyes of the world sport-loving public on whose favor the games ultimately depend.

The Role of Business

Business firms—seeking profit, prestige, or both—have long since become essential to the financing of the Olympics in the major non-Communist countries. Except where government was prepared to pick up the tab, this trend was inevitable, given the enormous growth in the size of the games and hence of their cost. From the 311 athletes and 42 events on the Athens program of 1896, the summer Olympics had grown by 1984 to include over 7,000 athletes in 223 events. The growth of the winter games has

The Seoul Olympic Stadium

Courtesy, Seoul
Olympic Organizing Committee

been proportional. The day is long past when private donations by a few wealthy men could enable a national Olympic committee to field a respectable team.

The cost to the host city has mounted similarly. After the 1976 summer games, Montreal found itself with a gaping $1 billion deficit. For the 1984 Olympic Games, a Los Angeles Olympic Organizing Committee was created six years ahead of time. Warned by Montreal's example, it held spending ruthlessly to under $500 million while taking in a spectacular $718.5 million. The biggest single item in the balance was the $225 million paid by ABC Television for exclusive U.S. broadcast rights.

And still the numbers mount. ABC paid $309 million for exclusive U.S. television coverage of the 1988 winter Olympics in Calgary. This, combined with record ticket sales and other commercial income, buoyed that Canadian oil-and-wheat metropolis after a long slump brought on by the sag in world prices for those two commodities. Such figures, compared with the estimated $1.2 million paid for TV rights at the Rome

Olympics in 1960, measure the spectacular growth in the popularity and commercial profitability of the Olympics—and, indeed, of all major international sporting events—during these three decades.

Governments Join the Game

Most formidable of all as a factor in the Olympic process—whether as supporters or as obstacles—are national governments. After World War I, and even more so after World War II, governments increasingly took note of the popularity of international sporting events, especially the Olympics, and began to make political use of them. In many countries—although conspicuously not in the United States—government ministries of sport appeared and started programs to identify and train promising athletes. Increasingly, too, governments applied their own foreign policy criteria to issues of participation by athletes from countries whose status was in dispute—Germany, China, Israel, Korea, Rhodesia and, in the most prolonged controversy of all, South Africa.

The results, from the standpoint of sport, were both positive and negative. On the positive side, governmental backing assured a high level of athletic prowess, aimed at the prestige that goes with Olympic gold. This helped greatly to raise the quality of competition worldwide—as statistics of new world records set in the Olympics clearly show. On the negative side, there was a great increase in governmental intrusion into the sport world—a trend not always compatible either with sport-for-profit or with sport-for-sport's-sake.

The IOC, to be sure, is not entirely without leverage. Its strongest lever, aside from the sheer prestige of the Olympic Games, is the power to decide where the quadrennial summer and winter Olympics shall be held. But the raw truth is that the IOC needs governments more than they need it. Time and again, when it suited their political purposes, they have used against the Olympics the most devastating weapon of all: boycott, or the threat of it. Seldom has the IOC imposed any penalty on a boycotting government.

Below the Olympic Summit

Largely separate from this Olympic structure, yet often connected with it, are less-inclusive international sport organizations—a bewildering variety. There are regional games, each involving many sports—the African, Asian, Mediterranean and Pan American games. These are smaller editions of the Olympics, held under IOC auspices every four years, a year or two ahead of the Olympic cycle. Each in its region serves, among other things, as a dress rehearsal for the next Olympics. A World University Games organization holds quadrennial multisport festivals for college and university teams the world over. Many federations hold single-sport world championship tournaments in basketball, ice hockey, swimming, table tennis, etc.—the most popular being the quadrennial World Cup soccer championship.

Other patterns abound, some multisport, others for one sport only. There are subregional games on the Olympic model in the Caribbean and among the five Association of Southeast Asian Nations members. The Commonwealth Games include most countries of the 48-member Commonwealth of Nations. Tennis has its venerable Wimbledon and Davis Cup tournaments and, in a recent development, separate tournaments promoted by business firms. Countless golf tournaments, bicycle and auto races, marathons, etc., are open to international competition. Yachting boasts the famous America's Cup race dating from 1851 and separate organizations for different racing-boat classes. And there are innumerable bilateral arrangements—annual U.S.-Soviet track and field meets, prizefights, exhibition games between American and Japanese or Cuban baseball clubs, and the like.

All such events, like the Olympics, are subject to manipulation by governments. An event can be cancelled or boycotted to show displeasure; or, conversely, improvised—like China's famous ping-pong gesture in 1971—to signal a desire for warmer relations. A recent example of the latter sort occurred in 1986 when the Soviet Union, in a move to end the U.S.-Soviet chill caused by the 1980 and 1984 Olympic boycotts, joined with the American TV entrepreneur Ted Turner to produce in Moscow a quasi-Olympic festival called the Goodwill Games. Attended by many ranking American athletes, the affair lost money but generated enough enthusiasm, political or athletic or both, to justify plans for a sequel in Seattle in 1990.

4

Who Plays? Who Pays?

Growth is never entirely painless. For the IOC and other institutions of world sport, the growing pains during the post-World War II decades arose in large part from two closely interrelated sets of issues:

▶ What standards, aside from athletic prowess, must an athlete meet in order to be allowed to play in Olympic sports? Shall the original Olympic ideal of the amateur athlete be retained, watered down, or dropped altogether?

▶ How are the ever-expanding Olympic and other international sport festivals to be paid for? Specifically, what financial role shall television and other commercial interests play, and what influence on the games will they acquire as a result?

Amateurs and Professionals

The idea of the accomplished amateur—in sport, music, or whatever—has always had an aristocratic, even slightly snobbish, ring to it. The word itself is French, and means literally one who loves; but it has come to mean one who performs solely for love and never for money—and who, by implication, doesn't need the money.

Allen Guttmann traces the amateur concept back five centuries to the Italian Renaissance, when a man of wealth and high station took pleasure in developing his talents in numerous fields—whence arose the term Renaissance man. Such a man in his youth was England's King Henry VIII, powerful in mind and body, equally able to compose music and (it was said) catch and subdue a deer with his own hands.

For de Coubertin and his friends amateurism was a meaningful concept, for when the Olympics began in 1896 professionalism was already widespread in European sports. Almost from the outset, however, the IOC found the amateur principle difficult to enforce or even define. As early as 1905 the IOC insisted that an Olympic athlete must be an amateur in all sports, not just the one in which he was competing in the Olympics. In 1925 it decreed that an amateur is "one who devotes himself to sport for sport's sake without deriving from it, directly or indirectly, the means of existence. A professional is one who derives the means of existence entirely or partly from sport." Before World War II the IOC fiddled again and again with the meaning of this rule, usually to tighten its application. Once, in 1927, it approved payment to athletes for "broken time"—time spent away from the job to train for or participate in the Olympics—only to reverse itself in 1930 and ban the practice. It also decided that whoever teaches a sport professionally is not an amateur—and refused to relax this decree when appealed to by the international ski federation. But the issue would not die. In the years just after World War II, the IOC stand against professionalism seemed more and more like King Canute forbidding the tide to advance.

The King Canute role in this issue—among others—was played with particular vigor by Avery Brundage, then head of the U.S. Olympic Committee. When Brundage's turn came in 1952 to be president of the IOC—the post he was to hold for 20 years—he made amateurism the theme of his inaugural speech. The principle, he said, was "universal, . . . rigid and unvarying, and cannot be changed. . . ." He continued to insist that an athlete who has ever been paid for engaging in any sport may not perform in the Olympics even in a different sport. He denounced the spreading practice of paying Olympic athletes to endorse commercial products. He displayed, in Guttmann's words, an "extraordinary if not wacky" zeal for stamping out the commercial use of the famous five-ring Olympic symbol. Only in 1971, the year before the 84-year-old Brundage retired, did the IOC overrule its chief and somewhat relax its controls over equipment advertising, commercial payments to athletes, and permissible training periods.

This concern had roots in Brundage's character and life story. The son of a stonecutter, raised in genteel poverty, he had made his own fortune in the Chicago construction industry. He was well-known in that bribe-ridden business as rigorously honest. As a young amateur athlete in track and field events, he became as strongly committed as any European nobleman to the Coubertian vision of amateur sport—a virtuous world apart. He was in his early thirties at the time of the "Black Sox" baseball scandal of 1919–20, in which a grand jury found that players for the favored Chicago White Sox had taken bribes to lose the World Series. To a man of Brundage's turn of mind it was a dire warning of what can happen when sport becomes sport-for-profit.

In perspective, it is easy to see the fatal weaknesses in Brundage's view.

▶ How could any country excel in world competition if most of its brilliant athletes—its Jim Thorpes and Jesse Owenses—were barred because they were too poor to compete as amateurs?

▶ How were unpaid amateur athletes from the West to compete with the state-trained, state-subsidized athletes of other countries?

▶ And how could the Olympics maintain their popularity and increase their global reach unless the world's greatest athletes, whether amateur or professional, were allowed to compete?

Despite Brundage's rigid stand, the tide in the IOC on the amateurism question had already begun to turn before his retirement. A 1969 IOC study on the issue concluded: "Olympic level performances cannot be any more realized by practicing sport as a game, or only for relaxation." Thereafter, the old position was yielded one step at a time on the insistence of the national Olympic committees and international federations. Under the pragmatic presidency of Juan Antonio Samaranch of Spain, an accomplished diplomat, the IOC has conceded to the sport federations its former role as rule-maker and policeman of amateur standing. In 1981, the IOC decided to let each federation define the word "amateur" for its particular sport—subject to an IOC approval which was most unlikely to be denied. "I'd like to see the [Olympic] Games more open," said Samaranch in a 1984 interview, "so that all the world's best athletes have a chance to compete." In 1986 the IOC executive board accepted recommendations from several federations that, among other things, permit—

✓ track and field teams to include "professionals in other sports";

✓ professional riders to compete in Olympic equestrian events;

✓ any ice hockey player approved by the international ice hockey federation, "including those who have or are presently playing as professionals for the National Hockey League (NHL) of North America," to play ice hockey;

✓ tennis stars—professional or not—to play provided they are not paid for doing so and, beginning two weeks before the Olympic Games, suspend all commercial endorsement contracts.

Amateur standing is not the only IOC eligibility rule to suffer gradual erosion. Another is the rule that a country's team shall consist only of nationals of that country. It is often circumvented by governments that improve their Olympic prospects by granting citizenship to star athletes from abroad. The United States itself, with the Olympics in view, has more than once taken steps to make "instant Americans" of athletes from Eastern Europe and the Soviet Union. For example, as this was written, legislation was pending in Congress to make a citizen of Ivan Lendl, the world tennis champion from Czechoslovakia, in time for the 1988 Olympics.

More Games, More Costs

"The [Olympic] Games have become 'Big Business' with obvious danger to Olympic ideals," wrote Brundage in 1958 in a note to the international sport federations. The immediate cause of his vexation was a report that the organizing committee for the summer Olympics in Rome that year would spend about $30 million, then an unheard-of sum for an Olympic host city.

Ever since becoming IOC president, Brundage had striven to curb costs by reducing the number of Olympic sports and the number of events in each sport. He correctly foresaw that if Olympic programs continued to expand, commercial financing would be unavoidable. He further believed, correctly or not, that corruption would certainly result. Therefore, the games must be cut back. His biggest targets for abolition were team sports such as basketball and soccer—two of the world's most popular sports—and the winter Olympics. On the other hand, he spoke up for women's events (but not for female shot-putters, whose muscularity offended him). These were not surprising choices for Brundage, who took pride in having competed in the 1912 Olympics in three solo sports (decathlon, pentathlon and discus), who had an eye for feminine beauty, and who was not quick to appreciate what he had not directly experienced.

But this was another battle Brundage was bound to lose. The gymnastic, boxing, swimming and other federations in the Olympic system constantly pressed for still more, not fewer, events in their respective sports. And new federations arose in such sports as team handball, volleyball and judo, all clamoring for Olympic recognition. The process continues to this day. At both summer and winter Olympics it has for many years been an established practice for the IOC and the host committee to schedule, in addition to the established "medal" sports, additional events in two "demonstration" sports which, if well received, will become part of the regular Olympic program four years later. In this fashion tennis, for the first time since 1924, was scheduled to rank as a medal sport at the 1988 summer games. Table tennis was to make its first appearance in the same year without going through the demonstration phase—an unusual concession to the South Korean hosts and their Asian neighbors, who excel at the game. And two demonstration sports—American baseball and tae kwon do, Korea's ancient martial-arts sport—were included on the Seoul program. If well received, they may be medal sports at the

Olympics in Barcelona, Spain—Samaranch's hometown—in 1992. Baseball's prospects, especially in Europe, are being promoted by, among others, Peter Ueberroth, the czar of the Los Angeles Olympics who is now U.S. baseball commissioner, and A. Bartlett Giamatti, an avid fan of the game, who went from the presidency of Yale University to the presidency of the National League.

Even in Brundage's day, the pressure that led to this expansion came not only from the sport federations but from within the IOC itself. A principal advocate was Konstantin Andrianov, the senior IOC member from the Soviet Union, whose country had entered the Olympic system in 1951. He charged that Brundage wanted to shrink the program to favor the United States at Soviet expense. He had a tactical ally in Britain's Marquess of Exeter, who was also president of the International Amateur Athletic Federation, a powerful body governing all track and field sports. In 1956 Exeter proposed, rather than curtail the Olympic program, a 5 percent surcharge on Olympic tickets—the proceeds to be divided between the federations and the IOC. But as things turned out, Exeter's tax—which Brundage adamantly opposed—proved unnecessary, for soon relief came from an unexpected quarter.

The TV Revolution

Television was only beginning to hit its stride in the mid-1950s, with color TV and satellite relays still in the future. Not until the Rome Olympics of 1960 could the organizers of the Olympic Games command a price for television rights. The total they then received from all broadcasters was approximately $1.2 million, of which a mere $400,000 was from the United States—tiny amounts by today's standards. What happened after that is shown in the table compiled by the U.S. Olympic Committee.

Ticket sales, commercial sponsorships, sales of Olympic coins, posters, and the like, had been increasingly relied on as costs rose. But no other source could approach TV in magnitude. As a result, the TV industry, and especially the American networks, became a major presence in the world of sport.

Winter Games TV Coverage*

Year	Location	Network	Amount Paid
1960	Squaw Valley, Calif.	CBS	$50,000
1964	Innsbruck, Austria	ABC	$597,000
1968	Grenoble, France	ABC	$2.5 million
1972	Sapporo, Japan	NBC	$6.4 million
1976	Innsbruck, Austria	ABC	$10 million
1980	Lake Placid, N.Y.	ABC	$15.5 million
1984	Sarajevo, Yugoslavia	ABC	$91.5 million
1988	Calgary, Alberta, Canada	ABC	$309 million

Summer Games TV Coverage*

Year	Location	Network	Amount Paid
1960	Rome, Italy	CBS	$394,000
1964	Tokyo, Japan	NBC	$1.5 million
1968	Mexico City, Mexico	ABC	$4.5 million
1972	Munich, West Germany	ABC	$7.5 million
1976	Montreal, Canada	ABC	$25 million
1980	Moscow, Soviet Union	NBC	$87 million
1984	Los Angeles, Calif.	ABC	$225 million
1988	Seoul, South Korea	NBC	$300 million

*For U.S. rights only. Payments for the U.S. rights in both 1984 and 1988 accounted for more than three quarters of the total paid by broadcasting agencies worldwide.

Has the impact of TV been good or bad? A good deal of both seems the only fair answer. Television, its reach enormously extended by satellite relay, can be seen and heard by as many as 2 billion people throughout the world. In North America and much of Europe, and especially in the United States, it addresses viewers both as sports fans and as consumers. At one stroke it has solved the financial problems of the still ostensibly amateur Olympic system, and thus has made possible the great increase in the number of Olympic events that can be staged and (provided good taste is in command) the elegance of the production.

These benefits are not cost-free. Many fans in the Western world are put off by the relentless commercial intrusions into Olympic programming on TV. A quite different charge is that the American networks—indeed, all the U.S. news media—pander to raw American patriotism, even chauvinism, in their Olympic coverage. They routinely give special coverage to American competitors whether or not they come close to winning medals. Sometimes they even influence the organization and scheduling of events such as the hockey tournament at Calgary in 1988 which, according to *The New York Times,* was "expanded from 8 to 12 teams for the first time [in winter Olympic history], presumably to keep a so-so American team alive for ABC for as long as possible" during the three-weekend festival. A far worse scheduling headache, however, faced NBC in planning coverage of the 1988 games in Seoul: namely, whether the hosts, in a time zone nine and a half hours from New York City, could be persuaded to schedule the events Americans like best at hours that make possible live U.S. broadcast in prime time.

How seriously do charges of American chauvinism and American manipulation deserve to be taken? IOC president Samaranch, interviewed by *The Los Angeles Times* just after the 1984 summer games, took a tolerant view of the matter. He pointed out that ABC, in addition to reporting the Los Angeles games for American viewers, had provided a "feed" to foreign TV services, allowing them "to tailor their coverage to events of interest to people in Japan, Great Britain and so on." And, he asked, "What is wrong with people feeling proud of the athletes who represent their countries? It's perfectly normal."

Samaranch might have added that most Americans get a better chance to applaud the greatest foreign performers—an Olga Korbut, a Pirmin Zurbriggen, a Carlos Lopes—by watching the Olympics on TV than in any other way. De Coubertin himself might not have been altogether displeased.

5

The Games of Power—
Under Which Flag?

The Olympic system has been caught in the middle of many a power play among nations since World War II. In states cut in two by opposing alliances—Germany, China and Korea—rival governments have battled for decades for Olympic recognition. The long and bitter Arab-Israeli conflict, the struggle between whites and nonwhites in southern Africa, the world reaction to the Soviet invasion of Afghanistan—all these have spilled over into the sporting arena. In the process, the institutions of world sport have all been fought over and reshaped.

Two Germanys

In 1949, four years after Germany's defeat in World War II, the Western and Soviet zones of military occupation were converted by their respective occupiers into two states: the Federal Republic of Germany (FRG) in the west and the Soviet-sponsored German Democratic Republic (GDR) in the east. The partition gave rise to parallel institutions in every field of national activity, including sports.

In the Olympic system the West Germans had the inside track at first, for the three occupying powers that had created their new state were also the dominant Olympic countries: Britain, France and the United States. Leaders of Germany's prewar national Olympic committee promptly revived that body, and in 1951— after a formal apology for Hitler's aggressions—obtained IOC recognition for it as representing simply "Germany." The name was consistent with Western policy at that time, which was still aimed at reunification of the German nation "in freedom."

The East German Communists and their Soviet patrons, on the contrary, showed every intention of making the partition of Germany permanent. Early in 1951 a national Olympic committee from the GDR asked for separate IOC recognition. After much debate the IOC offered a compromise: two separate German committees but a single team for Germany at the Olympics. The East Germans at first refused, but they soon reconsidered. In the Olympics of 1956, 1960 and 1964, an all-German team competed for Germany, flying a special flag and greeted musically with a special anthem—Beethoven's "Ode to Joy" from the Ninth Symphony.

The all-German pattern could not last, for there was no such state as Germany in postwar Europe and was not likely to be. The GDR, backed by its Soviet patron and by most of the big sport federations, persisted in demanding full and separate recognition. By 1968 the IOC had decided that after the Mexico City games (then about to begin, with two German teams like Siamese twins sharing one flag and anthem) the two Germanys would compete in the Olympics under their official names and with their own flags and anthems.

For the GDR, the timing of the change was critical, for it enabled East Germany to compete as a distinctly separate nation at the 1972 summer Olympics in Munich, West Germany. Then and ever since, GDR athletes—graduates of a high-priority scientific selection and training system—have been spectacularly successful. At the Munich games, East Germany, with barely over a fifth of Germany's population, won far more medals than the West Germans. The medal gap has continued ever since. At the Moscow games in 1980, the East Germans were the only near rivals to the Soviet Union, which exceeds East Germany in

Billboards on wheels: Greg Lemond (left), en route to winning the 1986 Tour de France, with Niki Ruttimann of Switzerland, in Nevers, France.

population by more than 16 to 1. In the eyes of the world's sport fans, these extraordinary achievements have done much to put the GDR on the map as a nation among nations.

One China or Two?

The Republic of China (ROC) under Chiang Kai-shek entered the Olympic system in 1932. (Chiang's aim was political: to prevent Japan's Chinese puppet state of Manchukuo from being invited to the Olympics.) When Chiang's defeated government was driven from the mainland in 1949 to the island province of Taiwan (or Formosa, as it was then called in the West), the new People's Republic of China (PRC) lost no time in acting to supplant its old enemy in the world of sport. It formed its own national Olympic committee and lobbied for an invitation to the Helsinki summer Olympics in 1952.

From then on, the battle of the two Chinas plagued the Olympics, as well as the regional Asian Games, with little letup for more than three decades. In the IOC as elsewhere, the vastly greater size of the PRC was balanced for a time by the ROC's seniority, its greater diplomatic experience, and the power of the United States, its chief backer. But the argument of universality told strongly in favor of the PRC, the actual government of 98 percent of the most populous nation on earth. The IOC, under heavy pressure from supporters of both sides, improvised one awkward compromise after another.

But nothing seemed to mollify the PRC, which in 1958 had walked out of the Olympic system and stayed out all through the years of the Cultural Revolution. Finally, in 1971, a more benign PRC treated the world to what may be history's most famous political use of sport: the "ping-pong diplomacy" in which an American table tennis team was welcomed in Beijing to signal the end of 23 years of Sino-American enmity. This episode, according to historian David B. Kanin, "did more to alter public perceptions of U.S.-China relations than any of the other signs" prior to President Richard M. Nixon's China visit in 1972.

Even then, the world of sport, reflecting the political world, remained split three ways on the China issue: pro-PRC, pro-ROC and "two Chinas." In 1975 the PRC formally requested recognition by the IOC, and demanded expulsion of Taiwan in the same breath. In July 1976, while the IOC was still juggling this hot potato, Canadian Prime Minister Pierre Elliott Trudeau, host to the Montreal Olympics then about to open, forced the IOC's hand by announcing that Taiwan athletes would not be admitted under a name containing the word "China." Despite loud objections from Washington, the IOC yielded, and the team from Taiwan, already in Montreal, went home rather than change its name.

Underlying all these maneuvers was a historic shift in China's geopolitical position. Its alliance with the Soviet Union had all but died by the early 1960s. By 1971 it was busily—and visibly—acquiring a new superpower friend, the United States, although the latter still paradoxically remained the chief protector of the "other China" on Taiwan. In these circumstances the decline of the ROC in world affairs became inevitable. The decisive event came on January 1, 1979, when the Carter Administration closed its embassy in Taiwan's capital, Taipei, and recognized the PRC as the sole government of China.

There were immediate consequences for the 1980 winter Olympics in Lake Placid. The IOC, still treading a narrow line, told the Taiwan committee to bring a new anthem and flag—or stay away. The Taiwan team, barred from the Olympic village, went to court in New York State but lost and departed. Taiwan was likewise barred from the summer Olympics in Moscow (where there was no Chinese team at all, Beijing having joined the boycott over the Afghanistan issue).

Since 1980 Taiwan has managed to retain membership in enough sport federations to assure itself continued IOC recognition under the curious name "Chinese Taipei," a formula the PRC seems willing to live with.

The PRC's overwhelming advantage in population over its compatriots on Taiwan was demonstrated at the 1984 summer games, where PRC athletes won 32 medals, including 15 golds, against 1 bronze medal for the Taiwan team. The PRC has world-class performers in women's volleyball, high jump, and— up to now—table tennis, which today ranks as an Olympic sport. But China still has far to go to realize its huge athletic potential. At an all-China sport festival in Canton in 1987, 18 world records fell, but only 3, all in weightlifting, were in Olympic events. Chinese sport authorities are determined to improve their showing at the Seoul Olympics and at the 1989 Asian Games, at which the PRC will be the host.

Whoever doubts that a serious commitment underlies these efforts should consider the fact that Beijing has already made known its wish to serve as host to the Olympic Games in that uniquely symbolic year, 2000.

6

Enter the Third World

Of all the changes in the world political map since 1945, none has been more momentous than the conversion of the vast colonial empires of the 19th century into the hundred-plus great and small nations of the Third World. Weak in power but strong in numbers, they pursued their goals—economic development, opposition to Western imperialism and an end to white racism, especially in southern Africa—in every available forum from the United Nations and the Nonaligned Movement to the Olympics and other organizations of international sport, some of which they created for the purpose.

One such Third World creature, strongly backed by the PRC and designed as a direct challenge to the Olympic system, was a sport festival known as Games of the New Emerging Forces, or GANEFO. It was the brainchild of President Sukarno of Indonesia, a politician bitterly hostile to the West.

The idea developed in 1962 when Indonesia, as host to the Fourth Asian Games to be held in the capital city of Jakarta that summer, denied visas to the athletes from two members in good standing, Taiwan and Israel. This action conflicted directly with the policy of the IOC, whose sponsorship is important to the regional games. Following the games, in further defiance of the IOC, Sukarno announced his sport festival plan involving the peoples of Asia, Africa, Latin America, China and the Soviet bloc. Such a festival, of course, would be under no compulsion to include Israel, Taiwan or any other outposts of "imperialism."

In February 1963 the IOC replied by suspending Indonesia's national Olympic committee. Undaunted, Sukarno withdrew Indonesia from the Olympic Movement and scheduled the first GANEFO for the following November in Jakarta. Invitations went out to 68 selected countries in Asia, Africa, Latin America, the Soviet bloc and even Western Europe.

Fifty countries sent teams to these games, including ten members of the Arab League and four non-Arab African countries. The largest team was that of the PRC, Sukarno's best friend, which took the lion's share of the medals. Moscow, already feuding with its Chinese ally, sent only second-string athletes. Other participants that valued their Olympic standing did likewise, for the IOC had decreed in advance that athletes who competed in Jakarta would be barred from the Tokyo Olympics in 1964.

Such a heavy Olympic reprisal may have been unnecessary, for with the overthrow of Sukarno in 1965 his plan for similar games in Cairo in 1967 fell of its own weight. The GANEFO dream was dead; but the episode could serve as a healthy warning to the Western-dominated IOC of what damage a Third World coalition, backed by a large disaffected power like the PRC, could inflict on an Olympic Movement insufficiently alert to Third World aspirations.

Arabs and Israelis: Boycotts and Murders

For Israelis perhaps more than for any other people, the words Olympic Games revive a searing memory: September 5, 1972, the day the Olympic village and the airport at Munich became the scene of a melodrama in which 11 members of Israel's Olympic team were taken hostage, then murdered, by Palestinian gunmen. It was the first—and as this is written, the only—such act of brutal violence in the Olympic Movement's history.

For Israel it was an atrocity demanding a visible reply, which took the form of air strikes three days later against Palestinian bases in Lebanon and Syria. For the West German hosts, it was a painful reminder of that ghastly chapter in Germany's history, the Jewish Holocaust. For all the powers involved in the long struggle between Israel and its Arab neighbors, it dramatized the new prominence of the militant Palestinian movement—and of a frightening method, terrorism.

That night the IOC leadership, after much bickering between the autocratic President Brundage and his colleagues, decided to continue the games after a day's delay for a memorial service in tribute to the Israelis. In his remarks following the service Brundage spoke what became his most famous words: "The games must go on." The Arab delegations, fearing retribution, quietly left Munich, and the games were completed one day behind schedule.

It was not the first time that the embattled state of Israel had found its place in the world of sport challenged by Arab foes. In 1948, in the midst of war with the surrounding Arabs, a newly formed Olympic Committee of Israel found time to "accept" the invitation which Britain, host to the Olympics that year, had sent to its predecessor, the Palestine National Olympic Committee. The Arab members threatened to boycott the games if Israel came, and Israel's committee was not recognized by the IOC until 1952. At the regional level Israel has waited much longer than that. In 1951 the Mediterranean Games, a new grouping supported by the IOC, excluded Israel from its first meet in Alexandria, Egypt. Four years later the Arabs induced Spain to cut Israel out of the second Mediterranean Games in Barcelona. When the IOC in 1962 decreed that its patronage for future regional games would be granted only if all countries in the region were invited, the Arab organizers proceeded without the IOC's blessing—and without Israel.

Israel has also suffered bilateral sport boycotts among leading nonaligned countries sympathetic to the Palestine Liberation Organization, notably India. In 1988, however, India conspicuously staged an Israeli-Indian Davis Cup tennis match in New

Delhi, in what some observers saw as Indian-style ping-pong diplomacy.

Ever since Munich, a tacit Arab-Israeli "Olympic truce" has prevailed in the Olympic Games. But vigilance against terrorism at the Olympics has increased since 1972 and was especially evident in the 1988 preparations in Seoul.

Southern Africa: Sport vs. Race

As the Nazi Olympics of 1936 showed, the IOC's rules— particularly that forbidding racial discrimination—can be flouted with impunity when the political will behind them is not very strong. For many years, the same truth applied to the sporting world's long struggles over relations with white-ruled South Africa and Rhodesia. But in the 1960s, with the worldwide spread of the Olympic Movement, the balance of political forces changed; and so did the results.

The Rhodesian conflict, although long and bitter, is now history. As late as 1964, Southern Rhodesia had taken part in the Olympics as a British colony. Its trouble began in 1965 when its ruling white minority, defying London, proclaimed a maverick white-ruled republic. Under heavy black African pressure— loudly resented by Brundage—Rhodesia was excluded from the Olympics from 1968 on. After more than a decade of guerrilla war and international pressure, the black majority took power in 1980 in a new republic called Zimbabwe. The IOC now recognizes Zimbabwe's national Olympic committee.

The much larger struggle over South Africa still goes on. South Africa has been described by sport authorities as one of the most "sports-mad" countries in the world. White South Africans competed in the Olympics as early as the London games of 1908 and won their share of Olympic medals. They also competed regularly with teams of the old white British Commonwealth and other predominantly white countries, including the United States.

These arrangements came under heavy pressure after World War II as a result of two historic developments. The first was the rise to power in South Africa in 1948 of the rigidly segregationist

National party, which imposed on the voteless nonwhite majority sweeping laws requiring racial separation (*apartheid*) in virtually all phases of the nation's life. The second, in direct contrast to the first, was the rapid decolonization of Africa.

Year in and year out black Africans pressed their case for ending South Africa's suppression of the rights of its black majority in every available forum, including the organizations of international sport. In so doing they had the support of nearly all Third World countries and the Soviet bloc. South Africa's white rulers in Pretoria, the administrative capital, on the other hand, could extract no better than a vacillating and embarrassed defense from Britain, the United States and other former imperial powers.

In this predicament the South African government gradually evolved a split-level policy. Abroad, concessions were improvised whenever necessary to avoid international ostracism, especially from the Olympic system. At home, with rare exceptions, apartheid in sport was kept intact. (One exception, involving the champion golfer Papwa Sewgolum, an ethnic Indian, had an awkward outcome. In 1963 he was permitted to compete in, and won, South Africa's national open, defeating Gary Player and other ranking whites. He was handed his trophy through a clubhouse window as he stood in the rain while his defeated competitors took their ease inside.)

Black Africa Takes the Lead

The 1960 games were the apartheid state's last hurrah in the Olympics. In that crucial year, a massacre of black demonstrators in Sharpeville, South Africa, shocked the world into awareness of apartheid; and 16 European colonies or protectorates in Africa were granted independence, with more soon to follow.

From then on a cascade of events put South Africa and its white sport organizations increasingly on the defensive. In 1960 France and the states of its former African empire organized a sport festival called the *Jeux d'Amitié*, open to any African state except South Africa. In 1961 South Africa withdrew from the British Commonwealth, already dominated on racial issues by its non-

USIA

Abidjan, Ivory Coast: Olympic gold medalist Lee Evans instructs athletes at a 1984 pre-Olympic training camp sponsored by the United States Information Agency's Sports America program.

white majority. The world football (soccer) federation suspended its South African affiliate. In 1962 a new group, the South African Nonracial Olympic Committee, arose to challenge the South African National Olympic Committee's credentials and further isolated South Africa in the sport world. When the Pretoria government stiffly reaffirmed its rejection of racially mixed teams, the IOC, getting tough at last, warned South Africa to get the policy changed or be suspended. South African concessions were too little and too late. In January 1964 the IOC voted to withdraw its invitation to South Africa to the Olympics in Tokyo that summer.

It was the first Olympics without South Africa, but not the last. Several more sport federations expelled South Africa. Demands for its ouster from the Olympic system were made in 1965 by a conference of 80 national Olympic committees meeting in Rome. In 1966 a Supreme Council for Sports in Africa (SCSA) was formed by 32 African states—and soon became the focal point in the struggle against apartheid in sports.

By this time the IOC leadership had begun to worry lest black Africa walk out of the Olympic system into a group such as GANEFO. It continued to press the South Africans to conform to the IOC rule on nondiscrimination. South Africa responded by offering to send a racially mixed team to the 1968 Olympics. In February 1968, Brundage and the other IOC leaders, dismissing threats from the SCSA of a mass African withdrawal, decided to admit the proposed mixed South African team to the Mexico City games.

It was a tactical blunder. Within days the threatened withdrawal of African teams from the Mexico Olympics was under way. Many other countries were reported ready to follow suit. The desperate Mexican hosts begged Brundage to reconsider. When he flew to Johannesburg to suggest privately that South Africa withdraw, Frank Braun, the South African National Olympic Committee chairman, replied that he "would rather be shot in Mexico City than lynched in Johannesburg." So the IOC, facing reality at last, voted to "advise" South Africa to stay away because of the "international climate." The South Africans submitted; the African boycott was lifted; and the Mexico City games were saved.

From then on South Africa's position in world sport went steadily downhill. When predominantly white countries were invited to the "South African Games" in 1969, black Africans threatened to boycott the Commonwealth Games and the Munich Olympics. Nearly all those invited declined. South Africa found itself frozen out of one sport federation or international athletic event after another. In May 1970 the IOC expelled South Africa from the Olympic Movement. It was the first such step in Olympic history.

The Africans, unrelenting, focused their attack on countries whose athletes play games with South Africans. In May 1976, as a New Zealand rugby team was preparing for a South African tour, the SCSA announced a black African boycott of the Montreal Olympics that summer unless New Zealand was banned from participating. The IOC, correctly under its rules, refused to budge—and 30 African countries stayed away from

Montreal. It was a sad day for track fans and especially for Tanzania, whose Filbert Bayi was the only runner alive in a class with New Zealand's John Walker in the 1,500-meter event. Walker won, but his victory had lost much of its meaning.

Underlying the Olympic struggle over South Africa was a basic misunderstanding on the nature of the issue. To the IOC majority, the only question before them was whether South Africa complied with Olympic principles. They judged that it had done so by its 1967 concession. But the African members, speaking through the SCSA, were not playing by Olympic rules. They were determined to force changes in South Africa's conduct in all sports and, indeed, in all aspects of race relations. They viewed the Olympics, along with diplomacy, trade and guerrilla war, as one more arena in a total war on apartheid. Until apartheid is ended, they said in effect, the world of sport must put its practitioners, and those who play games with them, beyond the pale. As late as the spring of 1988 there were threats of an African boycott of the Seoul Olympics unless countries whose teams play rugby with South Africans were excluded.

The IOC: Decline of the 'Tin Gods'

A major effect of the South African trouble was a public display of the weakness of the IOC. Brundage himself, for all his bluster, was well aware that the Olympic system could not afford to alienate black Africa. In 1976, after his time, the IOC imposed no penalty on the 30 boycotting African nations; and although it later threatened to suspend any boycotting country from the games for five years, the threat was never carried out.

These events can be seen as part of a larger pattern. In world sport as in world politics, the entrance of the Communist powers and of the Third World on the international stage powerfully affected long-established institutions. In particular, they accelerated the steady leakage of authority from the IOC to the sport federations and the national committees—and through them to the sovereign governments which, Olympic ideology notwithstanding, could dominate their supposedly autonomous national committees whenever political convenience required.

In 1959, with a crisis brewing over Brundage's opposition to new Olympic financing, the Soviets proposed to dilute the 64-member IOC by adding to it the heads of 35 federations and of the 115 national committees—more and more of which were closely monitored by their governments. No longer, under the Soviet plan, would the summit of the Olympic system be dominated by a self-perpetuating, Europe-centered rich man's club; and no longer could it even pretend to be immune to governmental influence.

The IOC overwhelmingly voted down the Soviet proposals. But Moscow persisted, and thereby won much goodwill among Third World leaders and others excluded from the IOC inner circle. By the mid-1960s, the Third World countries were engaged in a rebellion of their own.

At the head of this effort was Giulio Onesti, leader of the Italian Olympic committee. Again, money was a main factor. Onesti pressed for regular national committee meetings with the IOC executive board to discuss TV revenue and other issues. Getting nowhere with the IOC ("Let them talk, then forget it," Brundage advised an American colleague), Onesti in 1965 convened a caucus of 68 national committees which demanded 25 percent of Olympic TV revenue and launched a new organization, the Permanent General Assembly of National Olympic Committees.

This new organization conducted a vendetta against the IOC for several years. Feelings at times ran high. Once, after a typical Brundage brush-off, Khaw Kai-Bow, Malaysia's representative, denounced the IOC to its face as a band of "tiny tin gods— incommunicado to all and sundry." Brundage's inflexibility briefly drove 22 European IOC members into the camp of the Permanent General Assembly. But by 1969 the assembly had passed its peak, defeated by its own leaders' jockeying for personal power. Also, it soon had a rival, the General Assembly of International Federations, a parallel organization founded in 1967, which wanted a third of the TV money for its members.

The three-cornered maneuvers continued for years, but no major solutions emerged until Brundage's reign as IOC president ended in 1972. Under his successor, Lord Killanin of Ireland, the IOC quickly made peace with the national committees and federations and established an Olympic Solidarity fund to give technical aid to sport programs in the developing countries—the money to come from the national Olympic committees' share of the host country's TV revenue.

In addition, the three organizations in 1973 sponsored a much-postponed Olympic Congress, the first since 1930. The congress became a sounding board for the grievances of Olympic athletes, including especially women athletes. The athletes as a whole gained little more than a chance to air their grievances, but the women's pleas eventually had some effect. Until then the IOC had never had a woman member; by 1987 its 90 members included 5 women—a modest improvement. And from 1972 to 1984 the percentage of women among the athletes at the summer Olympics rose from 14 to nearly 30.

The national committees and sport federations could claim more. Out of the confrontations of the 1960s they had gained a far more influential place in the Olympic system and the world of sport. The IOC, for its part, remains supreme in the selection of Olympic host cities. On other issues, notably the sharing of increasingly lucrative TV revenues, it has ceased to claim supreme authority and serves as a center for negotiated solutions. Again and again it has threatened boycotting countries with exclusion from the Olympics and has warned countries that deny visas to qualified athletes on political grounds that they could forfeit their host-country privileges; but these punishments have rarely been applied. Essentially, the IOC is the UN of sport—not the master of the Olympic powers but their indispensable servant.

7

Superpower Sport:
Cold War and Détente

After World War II the Soviet Union, for the first time since the Bolshevik Revolution, began to play a significant part on the world sport scene. In 1951 the IOC recognized the Soviet national Olympic committee and, in addition, elected two Soviet sport officials to IOC membership. To take these steps the IOC leaders had to swallow not only their dislike of communism and of the Soviet officials' confrontational style, but the obvious inconsistency of the Soviet system with Olympic principles on amateurism and on freedom from government control. They may well have reasoned that the Soviet Union must either be accommodated or become the center of a potent rival to the Olympic system. As the IOC president of the time, Sigfrid Edstrøm of Sweden, delicately put it, "Our young athletes all over Europe are crazy to have the Russian athletes participate."

When Soviet teams made their Olympic debut at Helsinki in 1952, the Korean War was still raging and the first North Atlantic Treaty Organization (NATO) military buildup in Europe was being planned. The Soviet teams were housed separately, insulated from the camaraderie of the Olympic village. In the games themselves, the blend of ideology with normal competitiveness made a heady brew for superpower athletes and their fans. The American decathlon champion Bob Mathias recalled the Russians at Helsinki as "in a sense the real enemy. You just loved to beat 'em. You just had to beat 'em. It wasn't like beating some friendly country like Australia." Each side devised its system of national point scores—a concept abominated by Olympic purists—to prove that it had "won" the games.

Through more than three decades since Helsinki, the U.S.-Soviet rivalry has been for countless millions the emotional highlight of the Olympics. Despite the crude chauvinism involved, the result has been partly constructive; for the feeling of "us against them," when added to the formidable athletic prowess of the superpower teams, has undoubtedly widened the popularity of the Olympics in the age of mass TV audiences.

Afghanistan's Long Shadow

In 1974, when the IOC picked Moscow over Los Angeles as host city for the 1980 summer games, its primary reason was that it was high time for the games to be held in the Soviet Union, already a major Olympic power for two decades.

There were numerous objections in the West. Israelis and Jewish organizations were indignant, recalling an obviously officially staged anti-Semitic episode at the 1973 World University Games in Moscow. But the IOC stuck to its decision—swayed in part by the Soviet promise of security against terrorism. The Americans were mollified by the choice of Lake Placid for the 1980 winter games.

No one then could have foreseen that the Soviet Union, in the dying days of 1979, would launch a full-scale military invasion of Afghanistan. In the Third World as well as in the West, this act was denounced as naked aggression. President Carter, already sorely beset by the Iranian hostage crisis, had few options. His most dramatic response was a threat: Get out of Afghanistan or we will lead a general movement to cancel, move or boycott the 1980 Moscow Olympics.

The boycott idea proved popular in the United States. The

White House and State Department promoted it vigorously, both abroad and in the American sport establishment—but with mixed results. At home, heavy pressure was required to overcome the resistance of the U.S. Olympic Committee, which spoke for many world-class American athletes eager to compete against their Soviet counterparts. Abroad, the U.S. diplomatic corps managed to round up 62 countries for the boycott, including West Germany, Canada and Japan. But 81 countries went to the Moscow games—among them most of the NATO allies, most of Latin America (including Puerto Rico—proof of its independence in Olympic affairs) and the Third World.

When President Carter embarked on his boycott policy early in 1980, it had long since been settled that Los Angeles would be the Olympic host four years later. The Los Angeles organizers, with what they said was little or no help from Washington, did their best to encourage the Soviets to come, but to no avail. The entire Soviet bloc—minus Romania, the Warsaw Pact's maverick—stayed away, along with Cuba and a few other Soviet friends. Moscow blamed its boycott on inadequate security around Los Angeles, which may have been the truth—although many observers called it retaliation for 1980. When Romania's 127 athletes marched into the Los Angeles Memorial Coliseum on opening day, the American audience rewarded their defiance of Moscow with a delirious ovation.

Justified or not in political terms, the boycott and counterboycott of 1980–84 unquestionably hurt the Olympic Games—and the athletes most of all—by denying them the stimulus of competition with many of the world's greatest stars. This fact gave Olympic enthusiasts added reason to hope that the summer games of 1988 in South Korea would, for the first time in 12 years, include both superpowers and their main allies.

South Korea: Olympic Host, 1988

When the IOC in September 1981 chose Seoul, the Republic of Korea's sprawling capital, as the site of the 1988 summer Olympics, it was well aware of the political unknowns surrounding the choice. The nation had just begun to return to a state of relative calm after the two-year crisis following the assassination of President Park Chung Hee. And relations between the republic and Kim Il Sung's highly personal Communist dictatorship in North Korea remained dangerous, with intermittent bursts of violence. Who could tell what Korea would be like in another seven years?

However, the risks of the choice were outweighed by other considerations. Beginning in the 1960s, the IOC had sought as a matter of policy to include non-Western countries among the quadrennial Olympic hosts: hence Tokyo (1964) and Mexico City (1968). With the 1984 games in the United States, it seemed Asia's turn again. The only other city presenting itself was Nagoya, Japan. The IOC preferred Seoul partly because Japan had already had the summer Olympics in 1964 and the winter Olympics in 1972, but mainly because the IOC's scouts visiting Seoul had been amazed at the efficient and well-advanced preparations the city had already made. Since the 1960s South Korea had achieved extraordinary economic development. In athletics it still lagged far behind Europe, but it had built a serious sports training center—after failing to win a single medal at the 1964 Olympics—and was beginning to do better.

Athletically, at least, the IOC's confidence proved well placed. At the 1984 Olympics in Los Angeles the South Koreans took 19 medals, including 6 golds in boxing, judo and wrestling; and at the 1986 Asian Games in Seoul—the city's, as well as the region's, dress rehearsal for 1988—they did even better. The Seoul Olympics themselves would give a further shot in the arm to world-class sports not only in South Korea but throughout East Asia.

Still, two troubling questions remained:

(1) Would the Olympic show be ruined by political turbulence in South Korea? The omens were uncertain. In December 1987, after two years of protests and street battles against the military-dominated regime of Chun Doo Hwan, direct presidential elections—the first in many years—brought victory to Roh Tae Woo, Chun's candidate; but most of the votes were divided among his opponents. Parliamentary elections followed in April with simi-

lar results. South Korean politicians, unskilled in compromise, seemed headed for a new experience: coalition government. Pessimists could easily predict failure and a violent return to battle in the streets—possibly during the Olympics, a tempting world theater for political protest.

Optimists, on the other hand, could point to the South Koreans' natural patriotism, and their consequent reluctance to spoil the Olympic show and mar South Korea's world reputation. Even the often defiant opposition leader Kim Dae Jung had said: "We have no intention of embarrassing the South Korean government by exploiting the Olympic Games." Risks there were bound to be—but there was reason to hope that all concerned would put aside their quarrels until the games were over.

(2) Would the North Koreans try to sabotage the Seoul Olympics? The recent fatal bombing of a South Korean airliner over Southeast Asia, with evidence pointing strongly to North Korean authorship, suggested that the propensity for terroristic acts was still there. Conceivably they might be impelled to more of the same by the failure of their Olympic diplomacy. Their repeated demands that North Korea serve as equal cohost to the 1988 summer games had led in 1986–87 to counteroffers from the Seoul organizing committee: up to five Olympic sports (out of a total of 23) to be based wholly or partly in the North Korean capital, Pyongyang, instead of Seoul. North Korea had refused even to participate in the games on such terms, and negotiations in early 1988 seemed at an impasse.

The North Korean boycott threat had few backers. An all-time record 161 countries—including the Pyongyang regime's earliest patrons, the Soviet Union and China—had accepted the invitation to Seoul, while only Cuba, Nicaragua, Ethiopia and a handful of lesser countries held out. (Cuba's announcement started reports that the Pan American Games Organization might respond by rescinding its award of the 1991 Pan American Games to Havana, but it seemed doubtful that this threat would be carried out.) Olympic diplomacy between the two Koreas continued, with IOC president Samaranch doing his best to help—but all in vain.

In these circumstances it was not inconceivable that Pyongyang, out of sheer spite or some unfathomable calculation of political advantage, might find some way to attack the Seoul Olympics. Heavy security around Seoul, and a U.S. naval show of force around South Korea during the games, were planned as deterrents.

Except for the North Korean problem—and the nagging possibility of another African boycott over the old issue of rugby with South Africa—the outlook for Seoul in mid-1988 was bright. Taken together with the winter Olympics in Calgary, the Seoul games would make 1988 far and away the biggest year in Olympic history.

For the South Korean hosts, the promise of 1988 was greater still. For years, electronic signboards all over Seoul had flashed the number of days remaining before their president spoke the ritual words, "Let the games begin." Some $3 billion had been invested in building Olympic facilities in the Seoul area, many of which would be of permanent value to the city. Olympic contacts were being exploited to promote South Korean economic relations with China, the Soviet Union, Hungary, Vietnam and other countries. South Korean businessmen even spoke of their country joining the 24-member Organization for Economic Cooperation and Development, a developed-country "club" whose only Asian member is Japan. As the Tokyo Olympics of 1964 had marked a "new" Japan's emergence on the world stage, so the Seoul Olympics would mark the debut of South Korea as one of the world's important powers.

8

The United States in World Sport

During the Battle of the Bulge in December 1944, when Hitler's armies made their last desperate lunge against the Allied armies in Europe, a number of German soldiers, dressed in GI uniforms, infiltrated the Allied lines on sabotage missions. The men chosen had all lived in the United States and were fluent in American English. One trick the Americans used to unmask these plausible strangers was to ask them questions about the current baseball scene in the United States, such as whether St. Louis had won or lost the World Series that October. (Answer: Both. It was the only year both St. Louis teams won their league pennants. In the series the Cardinals beat the Browns 4 to 2.)

The story illustrates two facts about sports in the United States. One: most Americans take a lively interest in baseball. Two: few Europeans do, for this game—as well as American football—evolved in the United States and has never caught on in Europe. Only in the 1980s was baseball—which is popular in Japan and several Latin American countries—allowed demonstration tournaments in the Olympics. American football has yet to take root abroad except, in somewhat different forms, in Canada and Australia. Yet even today these two games, together with ice hockey and basketball (two other North American inventions), dominate the American sports diet.

True to the American tradition, these sports have never been, like yachting or polo, the preserve of the rich; they are the possession—some would say the obsession—of a whole nation. Many an immigrant or immigrant's child, and many a black American, has raised the pride of his or her ethnic peers through stardom in sports. The loyalty of each American toward one particular team is a standard theme in American humor. Richard Lipsky, a passionate basketball fan turned political scientist, has described his ecstasy as his beloved New York Knicks, after a long losing streak, became 1970 champions by beating the Los Angeles Lakers. The moment of victory, Lipsky writes, "was the emotional peak of my life."

Contemplating such facts, one might well ask: In this continental nation which thinks nothing of calling its national baseball classic the World Series, who needs international sports? But history has answered that question. The names of such Olympic prodigies as Jim Thorpe, Babe Didrikson, Jesse Owens, Mark Spitz, Dorothy Hamill and Carl Lewis have been as recognizable to American sports fans as those of any domestic football or basketball star. It is natural to want to see America's best tested against the world's best—whether for the love of sport or for reasons of patriotism, profit, foreign policy or sheer organizational momentum.

The story of the Pan American Games is a case in point. When war put a stop to the 1940 Olympics, Brundage, then head of the U.S. Olympic Committee, seized on an Argentine suggestion for a hemispheric sport festival as a way to keep the U.S. Olympic Committee busy and also to promote inter-American friendship. Plans to hold the first Pan American Games in Buenos Aires finally matured in 1951. Ever since, the games have been played on the same four-year cycle, one year before the Olympics, for which they provide regional preparation. The Indianapolis games in 1987—a bonanza for that city—were the 10th in the series. Next comes Havana, 1991—an occasion bound to shed new light on the troubled relations between Washington and the government of Fidel Castro. There appeared to be an understanding in advance of the 1987 games that if Cuba came to Indianapolis the Americans would go to Cuba's capital, Havana. The sending of 500 Cubans to Indianapolis seemed to be Castro's way of saying he expected the Americans to keep their promise.

The question, then, is not whether America will continue to play a major part in international sports, but how—and for what purposes. What part will be played by the U.S. government, either to facilitate or impede? Will government's aim be to win victories for patriotic and ideological reasons, or to win friends abroad through sport exchanges, or to serve foreign policy goals far afield from sport itself? The United States cannot abstain from these games of power; the best it can hope to do is to play them wisely.

Sports à la Tocqueville

Alexis de Tocqueville commented a century and a half ago in his *Democracy in America* on the American habit of forming associations for every conceivable purpose. It remains true today, and in no aspect of life more than in sports. The U.S. Olympic Committee, the private body that oversees U.S. participation in the Olympics and the Pan American Games, has 63 member organizations. Of these, 38 are single-sport groups representing amateurs (that is, those who meet the less and less strict Olympic definitions of the word) in every Olympic or would-be Olympic sport from archery to water skiing. Others are multisport bodies, the most powerful of which are the Amateur Athletic Union and the National Collegiate Athletic Association. Some groups foster sports for the handicapped. And all 50 states and the District of Columbia have Olympic organizations to help the U.S. Olympic Committee with fund-raising and public relations. Except for one group representing the U.S. armed forces (the IOC, in an exception to its rule on amateurism, has always allowed military personnel to compete), none of these organizations is subject to, or owes its existence to, the U.S. government.

Financially, too, the nation's activity in international sport, with some important exceptions discussed below, is in the private sector. Half of the U.S. Olympic Committee budget—which has escalated rapidly, and stood at $133.4 million for the four-year period 1985–88—is financed by American corporate sponsors through contributions of money, products and services. The balance comes from royalties on the licensed manufacture and sale of posters, pins, etc., bearing the U.S. Olympic Committee emblem; direct mail; efforts of the state-level affiliates; and, in a number of states, laws allowing taxpayers to share part of their tax refunds with the U.S. Olympic Committee. In addition, the U.S. Olympic effort benefits from a program in which companies provide Olympic athletes with jobs on terms that allow them time off to train and compete. The most important source of financing involving the U.S. government is the sale of Olympic coins, authorized by Congress and produced by the U.S. Mint. This program netted about $72 million in 1984, which the U.S. Olympic Committee and the Los Angeles host committee divided 50–50.

Private initiative played an even more dominant role when Los Angeles served as host to the 1984 Olympics. The story, told in detail by *Los Angeles Times* reporter Kenneth Reich, is unique in Olympic history. Mayor Tom Bradley and his city council, aware of the monstrous losses incurred by Montreal in the 1976 games, rejected a new IOC demand that the host city accept full financial liability. Private backers thereupon created a Los Angeles Olympic Organizing Committee, headed by Ueberroth, a self-made businessman and a tough negotiator. In partnership with the U.S. Olympic Committee, the Los Angeles committee agreed to accept financial liability provided the profits—few people expected any—would go to those who assumed the risk. It was the only hostship agreement the IOC had ever made with a private body. The outcome, what with Ueberroth's tight management and hard bargaining, and huge fees for TV rights, was an astonishing surplus of $222.7 million. The money was divided three ways: 40 percent to the L.A. committee; 40 percent to the U.S. Olympic Committee; and 20 percent to the latter's 38 sport affiliates. Since 1984 the bulk of these sums, plus smaller proceeds from the Olympic coin program, has been used to support amateur sports in the United States. The U.S. Olympic Committee used its share of about $115 million to set up an Olympic Foundation, half the income from which is spent on grants to the 38 member organizations—currently over $8 million a year—for use in their respective sports.

The Olympic Foundation's work supplements a program of the U.S. Olympic Committee that, for the last four years (1985–88), budgeted over $90 million for the support of athletics. The committee maintains three Olympic training centers in Colorado Springs, Colorado, Lake Placid, New York, and Marquette, Michigan. It makes grants for sports development; provides physiological, medical and rehabilitation services and drug counseling to athletes and trainers; supports sports for the handicapped; and conducts Olympic Festivals during non-Olympic summers in cities across the country. The festivals involve up to 4,000 athletes and serve as a showcase for Olympic aspirants. They have started numerous unknowns, such as the champion gymnast Mary Lou Retton, on their way to Olympic fame.

And Something for Friendship

Not quite all of the famous Los Angeles surplus of 1984 was spent inside the United States. Following a complaint by IOC President Samaranch that quarters for visiting teams in the Los Angeles Olympic village had been overpriced, the U.S. Olympic Committee, as cohost to the games, decided to defuse the issue by taking $4.2 million from its share of the surplus to establish a Friendship Fund for the training of coaches and athletic exchanges, chiefly with developing countries. The fund has not pacified the IOC but, according to the U.S. Olympic Committee, has been received appreciatively in participating countries.

Such Third World aid by the American sports community has long been dwarfed by the state-sponsored programs of the Soviet Union. Political scientist James Riordan, using Soviet sources, found a rapidly rising use of Soviet coaches as sport instructors in African and Asian countries beginning in the mid-1960s, with more than 200 coaches working in 28 countries in 1972. Sport centers had been built with Soviet aid in seven countries. Students from 25 Afro-Asian states had received coaching diplomas in the Soviet Union.

How Much Is Enough?

Are these sums enough? To reach meaningful answers, they must be viewed together with the many times larger sums spent on internationally recognized sports by American schools, colleges and amateur sport organizations, all of which play some part in the "feeder" system that produces world-class athletes.

Professional sports, the most richly financed, also have to be considered now that Olympic sports are increasingly open to professionals. But this is true only to a limited degree. Many a highly rated professional athlete, especially in team sports, is prevented by his or her contract from skipping a scheduled game for an unpaid Olympic appearance. Thus the top U.S. basketball players, all under contract to National Basketball Association teams, were not expected to play at the Seoul games. As for hockey, all but a few players in the NHL are Canadian citizens; thus the feisty but disorganized American team at the Calgary games in 1988 was made up of the best available college players—no match for the Soviet Union's best.

In any case, results, not dollars, are the true measure of sufficiency. Measuring the United States against the Soviet Union, Olympic statistics show that in the summer games of 1952 through 1972 the Americans won 214 gold medals to the Soviets' 211, while the Soviets in about the same period (1952–76) showed more "depth," winning 683 medals (gold, silver and bronze) to the Americans' 604. Such figures may suggest a rough equality, but the recent trend suggests otherwise. In their last Olympic encounter in 1976, the Americans, with 34 gold medals, were outstripped by the Soviets with 49, and even by the East Germans with 40. Americans remain supreme in track and field and in swimming and diving, holding 25 all-time Olympic records in these sports to the Soviets' 10. But Soviet athletes lead in gymnastics, weightlifting, wrestling and various sports not widely followed by Americans: handball, canoeing, kayaking, and women's volleyball, among others.

In the winter Olympics the superpower score has been one-sided from the beginning. From 1952 to 1984 the Soviet team took the most medals all but once (1968) when it lost out to Norway. But East Germany won nine golds to the Soviets' six in 1984. The United States has never come as close as second. At Calgary in 1988 the U.S. team, with only two golds and six medals in all, stood behind the Soviet Union and seven other countries—its all-time worst Olympic showing.

Sportswriters showed no surprise at such results, since Americans give most winter sports a lower priority than more northerly countries. Some commentators even wrote with feeling about the importance of knowing how to lose gracefully.

But the U.S. Olympic Committee was having none of such talk. Even before the Calgary games were over Robert H. Helmick, U.S. Olympic Committee president, announced the appointment of a seven-man Olympic Overview Commission headed by George Steinbrenner, principal owner of the New York Yankees. Its task was to find ways to improve the nation's Olympic performance in 1992 and thereafter.

The Steinbrenner commission had a full quota of questions. Does the "feeder" system by which promising U.S. athletes reach Olympic rank work effectively? Are American coaches up to date on winning techniques being used abroad? Is the United States doing enough to get sports in which Americans excel included in the Olympic schedule? Others put a further question: Is there some way by which the U.S. professional teams could free some of their stars to play for the Olympics?

Uncle Sam—Olympian of Last Resort?

Relations between the U.S. Olympic Committee and the government in Washington were also on the agenda of the new Steinbrenner commission. Traditionally, Washington's share in the nation's international sports role, whether at home or abroad, has been slight and, in some of its aspects, more negative than positive.

The negative side—the power of Washington to frustrate athletes to serve its diplomatic interests—was illustrated by its commanding role in the boycott of the 1980 Olympics. A smaller but more frequent irritant is the State Department's denial of visas on various grounds to foreign athletes, officials and journalists bound for sporting events on American soil. In March 1984 a Soviet Olympic attaché, assigned to Los Angeles to complete arrangements for the Soviet Olympic team, was refused admission, apparently on the ground that he was a KGB (Soviet secret police) officer. Among the Los Angeles hosts the belief lingers that the visa refusal was a factor in the Soviet decision to boycott the games.

On the positive side, where major sport festivals are held in the United States, Washington generally provides, in addition to the minting of Olympic commemorative coins, some special financing or its in-kind equivalent—such as money for site development at Lake Placid in 1980 or the free use of the U.S. Army's Fort Benjamin Harrison for the Pan American Games in 1987.

For many years a small trickle of money found its way into State Department projects to send American athletes and coaches on goodwill missions abroad, mainly to developing countries. Such projects began on a minute scale in the 1950s and reached their peak budgetary level in 1967—a mere $300,000. During two decades the money paid for about 165 tours abroad by American athletes, most of them to developing countries. At present, a comparable program called Sports America is administered by the U.S. Information Agency. It finances visits to developing countries by American coaches, sports-medicine specialists and athletes, and is budgeted at $330,000 a year (much less in purchasing power than the same figure in 1967). In addition, at no cost to the taxpayers, the agency facilitates athletic visits to this country from abroad.

Although reports of the Soviets' "sports diplomacy" provided the initial stimulus for such governmental programs, neither today nor at any time have they approached the magnitude of the Soviet programs in the Third World already described. Nor should they, for the Soviet approach is irrelevant to the American scene in which the private sector plays the dominant role. In addition to the U.S. Olympic Committee's Friendship Fund, countless American nongovernmental groups conduct a continuous traffic in athletic exchanges with foreign countries.

Yet a case can be made for a government program like Sports America, which tailors its projects to the needs of particular countries, and whose service to U.S. foreign policy is no more sinister than the creation of goodwill. Administering over 200 projects in its first three years, it has compiled numerous success stories that tell of friendships formed and valued contacts long after the initial visit. Ganiyu Otenigbagbe of Nigeria, after a four-week basketball clinic in Minnesota, wrote: "No one can ever again tell me anything about racism in the United States, because I will tell them about this man who opened his house for me." New Hampshire basketball coach Cecilia de Marco, two years after her assignment in Zimbabwe, was still sending her Zimbabwean friends boxes of used uniforms and athletic gear. Neil Richardson, the first American coach to visit Syria in 20 years, realized that basketball coaches and players misunderstood the basics of the game. He drilled them so tactfully, and so successfully, that the Syrians wanted to hire him—and a resident Soviet coach asked him for pointers. And in Mozambique, a country tormented by war and poverty, basketball coach Charles Skarshaug trained an underdog national basketball team so well that it won the East African tournament and made Skarshaug a national hero.

Should the U.S. government role in world sport expand much above the present level? Should the United States, like many other countries, formulate a national sports policy? Many an influential voice in past years has said yes to such questions. In 1962 Senator Hubert H. Humphrey (D-Minn.) proposed creation of a "private U.S. Olympic foundation" with the government paying the travel costs of Olympic teams. In 1965 General James Gavin, commissioned by President Lyndon B. Johnson to study the matter, recommended creation of a "National Amateur Sports Foundation" with mixed private and public financing. Both proposals were swallowed up in the Vietnam War emergency and have not been heard of since.

It seems unlikely that a tidy answer to this question will soon be arrived at, given our nation's highly diffuse style of public and private decisionmaking. But when and if the question is addressed, it will be important to think carefully about the fundamental values that sports serve and how well those values harmonize with the government's duty to conduct the foreign relations of the nation.

The Values of Sport

There is an ambivalence that pervades all human relationships—between cooperation and conflict, war and peace, the hunger for friendship and the hunger for power. It is as true in sport as in the relations among nations. The most important thing in the Olympic Games, affirmed the noble Baron de Coubertin, "is not to win but to take part"; and the American sportswriter Grantland Rice echoed him: "It's not whether you win or lose but how you play the game." But the combative pro football coach Vince Lombardi had a different view: "Winning isn't just the most important thing. Winning is the only thing."

A tenable position must lie somewhere between these extremes. It is the hope of winning that gives any game much—some would say all—of its savor. But some framework of rules must be respected, and the loser must at a minimum be allowed to survive—otherwise, what game would be left to win? Some more or less agreed framework of rules underlies every durable human arrangement, be it a marriage or an international alliance—or even an adversary relationship such as that between the superpowers. Having both realized in the nuclear age that they dare not make war on each other, both have been groping for ways to play the game of power without destroying the game and themselves with it.

In their calculations—and equally in those of other nations, intent on their own regional or local power games—sport is one of the minor instruments of statecraft. It can help to produce a warming or chilling of the atmosphere. Olympic historian David Kanin has correctly observed that sport is available for such purposes precisely because its victories and defeats are not physically dangerous. They are "*peripheral* to the international

67

system. . . . A defeat in a match will not normally be avenged by the use of force." Unfortunately for athletes and fans, this means that governments hold the power of life or death over international sport contacts.

In this situation it is evident that in determining the future of the Olympics the IOC, no matter how ably led, is as powerless to win a contest of wills against a sovereign state as is the secretary-general of the UN. However, the Olympics are in a less difficult position than the UN because their purpose is infinitely smaller and much more popular. There seems to be no nation on earth so pugnacious that its people, left to themselves, would be unwilling to take their hostile feelings to the Olympics or the regional games and try their chances on the playing field, win or lose.

Again and again in modern Olympic history, athletes from mutually hostile sovereignties—from both Germanys, both Chinas, both Koreas; Soviets and Americans, Cubans and Americans, Nicaraguans and Salvadorans, Arabs and Israelis, Indians and Pakistanis, Iranians and Iraqis—have contended together under the Olympic flag, playing by the rules of sport and not the rules of power. Their "sacred truce," like that in the Greek Olympics of old, extends only to the athletic arena, not to the world of national wars; but it is a genuine truce nonetheless, and is witnessed by sport fans the world over.

The historian William H. McNeill has written of a key question facing the dangerously overarmed community of nations: "how to define the limits of comradeship. . . . the boundary between 'us' and 'them'." He concludes that "the reality of world society" has rendered the world's inherited stock of national, ideological and sectarian myths inadequate; therefore, leaders of thought must rise "to the grandest mythical plane of which we are capable. Only so can the world we live in become intelligible." Perhaps it is not too much to hope that in the coming century the customs and images of the Olympic Games, along with the space-age vision of Planet Earth, may find a place in a new body of symbols and beliefs that can stir enough hearts to save humanity from itself.

Talking It Over

A Note for Students and Discussion Groups

This issue of the HEADLINE SERIES, like its predecessors, is published for every serious reader, specialized or not, who takes an interest in the subject. Many of our readers will be in classrooms, seminars or community discussion groups. Particularly with them in mind, we present below some discussion questions—suggested as a starting point only—and references for further reading.

Discussion Questions

For many years the leaders of the International Olympic Committee insisted that the Olympic Movement must remain "above politics," concerning itself only with sports. In reality, this quickly proved to be impossible. Why?

The rule admitting only amateur athletes to Olympic competition was established at the outset of the modern games in 1894. By the 1980s that rule had almost become a dead letter. What merit do you see in the original insistence on amateur standing?

In the early decades of the summer Olympics, American teams led those of any other country in the number of medals won. Since the 1950s the Americans have been surpassed several times by Soviet and even East German teams. What factors have caused this shift? How important is it, in your view, that the Americans should regain their supremacy—and what steps should be taken to that end? Do you have the same attitude toward the winter Olympics?

In light of the strong role of many governments in selecting, training and subsidizing their athletes for Olympic and other international competition, do you think the U.S. government should do the same? Explain your view.

From the "Nazi Olympics" of 1936 to the present, there has been bitter controversy over whether the Olympics and other international sport festivals should be open to countries whose governments violate human rights and other international norms of conduct. Do you think a general rule on this problem is possible? If so, what rule would you propose, and by what procedure would you apply it to particular cases?

Do you think international sport competition, as now conducted, contributes more to peace or to conflict among nations?

READING LIST

Ali, Ramadhan, *Africa At the Olympics*. London, England, Africa Books, 1976. Traces the rise of black Africa's sport movement and its war on South African apartheid.

Cumings, Bruce, "The Two Koreas." HEADLINE SERIES No. 269. New York, Foreign Policy Association, May/June 1984. Excellent account of the history and politics of North and South Korea. Good background for the 1988 Olympics.

Espy, Richard, *The Politics of the Olympic Games*. Berkeley and Los Angeles, University of California Press, 1979. A political scientist's thoroughly documented account of political issues in the Olympic system from World War II through 1980.

Gault, Frank, and Gault, Clare, *Stories from the Olympics*. New York, Walker, 1976. For younger readers: Olympic tales from Greek times to the present.

Greenberg, Stan, and others, *Guinness Book of Olympic Records*. New York, Bantam Books, 1988. Names and countries of medal winners (first three places) in summer and winter Olympics, 1896–1984.

Groussard, Serge, *The Blood of Israel: The Massacre of the Israeli Athletes*. New York, William Morrow, 1975. Dramatic, partly eyewitness story of terrorism at the 1972 Munich games.

Guttmann, Allen, *The Games Must Go On: Avery Brundage and the Olympic Movement*. New York, Columbia University Press, 1984. Life of the controversial American who dominated the IOC for 20 years, told with admirable historical insight.

———, *Sports Spectators*. New York, Columbia University Press, 1986. From Greco-Roman times to the TV revolution—a unique account and analysis of the fans' political and social role in world sport.

————, *A Whole New Ball Game: An Interpretation of International Sports.* Chapel Hill, University of North Carolina Press, 1988.

Hart-Davis, Duff, *Hitler's Games: The 1936 Olympics.* New York, Harper & Row, 1986. Excellent history of the 1936 Berlin games and the political struggle in Britain, the United States and the IOC that led to the Western decision to take part.

Kanin, David B., *A Political History of the Olympic Games.* Boulder, Colo., Westview Press, 1981. Kanin views claims that the Olympics are above politics as spurious; traces the movement's political fortunes since 1894. Detailed chapter on the 1980 boycott.

Lapchick, Richard E., *The Politics of Race and International Sport: The Case of South Africa.* Westport, Conn., Greenwood Press, 1975. How blacks in and beyond South Africa organized to turn the Olympic Movement against apartheid.

Lipsky, Richard, *How We Play the Game: Why Sports Dominate American Life.* Boston, Mass., Beacon, 1981. A New York basketball fan turned political scientist surveys America's sports mania.

Lowe, Benjamin, Kanin, David B., and Strenk, Andrew, eds., *Sport and International Relations.* Champaign, Ill., Stipes Publishing Co., 1978. Over 30 articles of lasting value, though uneven quality, on a wide range of international sport topics.

Lüschen, Günther, ed., *The Cross-Cultural Analysis of Sport and Games.* Champaign, Ill., Stipes Publishing Co., 1970. Chapters by sociologists and anthropologists on sports and games in different cultures, including primitive, the world over.

Plant, Gayle, ed., "The U.S.A. in the Olympic Movement." Magazine-size booklet, 72 pages, distributed by the U. S. Olympic Committee, 1988, with data on past and present U.S. Olympic participation.

Reich, Kenneth, *Making It Happen: Peter Ueberroth and the 1984 Olympics.* Santa Barbara, Calif., Capra Press, 1986. A vivid though critical account of Ueberroth's triumph as chief of the Los Angeles Olympic Organizing Committee.

Swaddling, Judith, *The Ancient Olympic Games.* Austin, University of Texas Press, 1984. Short account of the first Olympics from eighth century B.C. to Roman times; pictures show Greek and Roman art on athletic themes.

Tomlinson, Alan, and Whannel, Gary, eds., *Five-Ring Circus: Money, Power and Politics at the Olympic Games.* London, England, Pluto Press, 1984. Excellent chapters on Olympic commercialism, politics, TV, apartheid, women and the forgotten "workers' Olympics" pre-World War II.

U.S. Postal Service
STATEMENT OF OWNERSHIP, MANAGEMENT AND CIRCULATION
Required by 39 U.S.C. 3685

1A. TITLE OF PUBLICATION	1B. PUBLICATION NO.								2. DATE OF FILING
Headline Series	0	0	1	7	8	7	8	0	1/11/88

3. FREQUENCY OF ISSUE	3A. NO. OF ISSUES PUBLISHED ANNUALLY	3B. ANNUAL SUBSCRIPTION PRICE
January, March, May, Sept., Nov.	Five	$15.00

4. COMPLETE MAILING ADDRESS OF KNOWN OFFICE OF PUBLICATION *(Street, City, County, State and ZIP + 4 Code) (Not printers)*

Foreign Policy Association, 729 Seventh Ave., N.Y., NY 10019

5. COMPLETE MAILING ADDRESS OF THE HEADQUARTERS OF GENERAL BUSINESS OFFICES OF THE PUBLISHER *(Not printer)*

Same as above

6. FULL NAMES AND COMPLETE MAILING ADDRESS OF PUBLISHER, EDITOR, AND MANAGING EDITOR *(This item MUST NOT be blank)*

PUBLISHER *(Name and Complete Mailing Address)*

Foreign Policy Association, 729 Seventh Ave., N.Y., NY 10019

EDITOR *(Name and Complete Mailing Address)*

Nancy Hoepli, Same address as above

MANAGING EDITOR *(Name and Complete Mailing Address)*

None

7. OWNER *(If owned by a corporation, its name and address must be stated and also immediately thereunder the names and addresses of stockholders owning or holding 1 percent or more of total amount of stock. If not owned by a corporation, the names and addresses of the individual owners must be given. If owned by a partnership or other unincorporated firm, its name and address, as well as that of each individual must be given. If the publication is published by a nonprofit organization, its name and address must be stated.) (Item must be completed.)*

FULL NAME	COMPLETE MAILING ADDRESS
Foreign Policy Association	

8. KNOWN BONDHOLDERS, MORTGAGEES, AND OTHER SECURITY HOLDERS OWNING OR HOLDING 1 PERCENT OR MORE OF TOTAL AMOUNT OF BONDS, MORTGAGES OR OTHER SECURITIES *(If there are none, so state)*

FULL NAME	COMPLETE MAILING ADDRESS
No stockholders - a non-profit organization	

9. FOR COMPLETION BY NONPROFIT ORGANIZATIONS AUTHORIZED TO MAIL AT SPECIAL RATES *(Section 423.12 DMM only)*
The purpose, function, and nonprofit status of this organization and the exempt status for Federal income tax purposes *(Check one)*

[X] (1) HAS NOT CHANGED DURING PRECEDING 12 MONTHS
[ ] (2) HAS CHANGED DURING PRECEDING 12 MONTHS
(If changed, publisher must submit explanation of change with this statement.)

10. EXTENT AND NATURE OF CIRCULATION *(See instructions on reverse side)*	AVERAGE NO. COPIES EACH ISSUE DURING PRECEDING 12 MONTHS	ACTUAL NO. COPIES OF SINGLE ISSUE PUBLISHED NEAREST TO FILING DATE
A. TOTAL NO. COPIES *(Net Press Run)*	13,883	12,300
B. PAID AND/OR REQUESTED CIRCULATION 1. Sales through dealers and carriers, street vendors and counter sales	2,777	444
2. Mail Subscription *(Paid and/or requested)*	4,731	4,886
C. TOTAL PAID AND/OR REQUESTED CIRCULATION *(Sum of 10B1 and 10B2)*	7,508	5,330
D. FREE DISTRIBUTION BY MAIL, CARRIER OR OTHER MEANS SAMPLES, COMPLIMENTARY, AND OTHER FREE COPIES	500	500
E. TOTAL DISTRIBUTION *(Sum of C and D)*	8,008	5,830
F. COPIES NOT DISTRIBUTED 1. Office use, left over, unaccounted, spoiled after printing	5,875	6,470
2. Return from News Agents	-0-	-0-
G. TOTAL *(Sum of E, F1 and 2—should equal net press run shown in A)*	13,883	12,300

11. I certify that the statements made by me above are correct and complete

SIGNATURE AND TITLE OF EDITOR, PUBLISHER, BUSINESS MANAGER OR OWNER

Mark Callahan Dir. of Administration (212) 764-4050

PS Form 3526, July 1984 *(See instruction on reverse)*